THE FIFTIES REVISITED

AN AEROBIOGRAPHY

BY

PETER CAMPBELL

CIRRUS ASSOCIATES

PUBLISHED BY:
Cirrus Associates (S.W.),
Kington Magna,
Gillingham,
Dorset,
SP8 5EW UK.

© Peter G. Campbell 1990, 1994, 1999

First published 1990,
Revised edition 1994,
New revised edition 1999

All rights reserved. No part of this publication may be reproduced, stored in a retrieval system, or transmitted in any form or by any means, electronic, mechanical, photocopying or otherwise without the prior written permission of the publisher.

ISBN 1 902807 00 6

PRINTED IN ENGLAND BY:
The Book Factory,
35-37 Queensland Road,
London,
N7 7AH.

DISTRIBUTORS:
Cirrus Associates (S.W.),
Kington Magna,
Gillingham,
Dorset,
SP8 5EW UK.

COVER PHOTO: Fairey Air Survey's Dakota 4 G-ALWC in front of the control tower at Shoreham, 20th July 1954.
Photo: Author's collection.

DEDICATION

This book is dedicated to the memory of David Timmis, my closest friend throughout the forties and fifties, and latterly a pilot of outstanding ability, who lost his life in a tragic flying accident near Mere, Wiltshire on the 24th March 1990.

ACKNOWLEDGEMENTS

Air-Britain (Historians) Ltd, Air Officer Commanding & Commandant (RAF College Cranwell), Peter Amos, Ambrose Barber, Lewis Benjamin, Jean Buckberry, James Campbell, Peter Elliott (RAF Museum), Tim Foster, Joyce Honner, Michael "Mike" Jones, Michael Jones (Tiger Club), George Miles, Marion Rogerson, Mark Rogerson, Ann Tilbury, Alexander Timmis.

CONTENTS

FOREWORD		7
CHAPTER 1:	WARTIME MEMORIES	13
CHAPTER 2:	COTTESMORE DAYS (1945–1951)	17
CHAPTER 3:	LANCING DAYS (1951–1955)	33
CHAPTER 4:	A LIFETIME'S HOBBY BEGINS (MID-1952–MID-1955)	44
CHAPTER 5:	THREE WEEKS IN THE LIFE... (JULY 1955)	58
CHAPTER 6:	ELEMENTS OF TRANSITION (MID-1955–MID-1956)	66
CHAPTER 7:	A DEGREE OF PROGRESS (MID-1956–MID-1959)	71
CHAPTER 8:	MAINLY FAIR OAKS AND WISLEY (1955–1960)	80
CHAPTER 9:	MUSICAL NOTES (1955 ONWARDS)	89
CHAPTER 10:	TRANSPORTS OF DELIGHT (1955 ONWARDS)	94
CHAPTER 11:	ONE DEGREE OVER (1959–1960)	98

APPENDIX 1:	EAST ANGLIAN FLYING SERVICES (LATER OPERATING AS CHANNEL AIRWAYS) AT SHOREHAM	105
APPENDIX 2:	DETAILS OF TYPICAL CLUB-OWNED AIRCRAFT SEEN AT SHOREHAM DURING 1952-1955	106
APPENDIX 3:	AIRCRAFT AT SHOREHAM ON THE 22ND JUNE 1952	109
APPENDIX 4:	LINCOLNS SEEN OVER SHOREHAM DURING MAY 1953	109
APPENDIX 5:	AIRCRAFT SEEN AT RNAS FORD (1953–1955)	110
APPENDIX 6:	AIRCRAFT ATTENDING THE PASSING OUT PARADE AT CRANWELL, 28TH JULY 1953	112
APPENDIX 7:	AIRCRAFT SEEN AT GATWICK, 17TH NOVEMBER 1953	113
APPENDIX 8:	AIRCRAFT AT SHOREHAM DURING THE VISIT OF THE HUREL DUBOIS HD-31, 25TH-28TH MARCH 1954	113
APPENDIX 9:	AIRCRAFT SEEN AT RAE FARNBOROUGH, AIR CADETS' VISIT, 18TH MARCH 1955	114
APPENDIX 10:	AIRCRAFT SEEN AT CROYDON, 10TH MARCH 1956	115
APPENDIX 11:	AIRCRAFT OVERFLYING WOKING ON FAIRLY TYPICAL DAYS DURING THE MID-FIFTIES	116
APPENDIX 12:	AIRCRAFT AT THE WOBURN RALLY, 2ND MAY 1959	119

APPENDIX 13:	AIRCRAFT AT THE GOODWOOD MOTOR RACING MEETING, 18TH APRIL 1960	120
APPENDIX 14:	TIGER CLUB AIRCRAFT SEEN AT FAIR OAKS DURING 1957	122
APPENDIX 15:	AIRCRAFT PARTICIPATING IN THE FIRST TIGER CLUB AIR SHOW AT FAIR OAKS, 19TH JULY 1958	122
APPENDIX 16:	AIRCRAFT FLOWN IN BY THE AUTHOR BETWEEN 1950 AND 1965	123
INDEX:	(MAIN TEXT ONLY)	125

FOREWORD

This is the personal story of my childhood, adolescence and early adulthood during the postwar years between 1945 and 1960. But why should I bother to record the details of my formative years for others to read? After all, I lay no claim to being famous – nor would I want to be. I have done nothing particularly dangerous, illegal, immoral, fattening or involving millions of pounds, so will you be the slightest bit interested in reading of my experiences? I hope so, especially if you are at all interested in the social history of the period, or in aeroplanes in particular.

Perhaps I was privileged to be sent to a public school, Lancing College, during the 1950s – who knows? All I can say is that while I was there my future life, both working and social, was moulded, without my realising it at the time, into a pattern which was to not really change that much over all the years that have flashed past since. I remain confident that, had it not been for the proximity of Shoreham Airport, my life would have been very different in many ways; thus, almost unseen and unnoticed at the time, occur the serendipitous happenings that can so often shape a person's future.

Many of us look back with affection and nostalgia to the days of our youth, when our lives both at home and at school were to quite a large extent arranged for us; some consider those days as the best days of their lives. For children growing up through the second World War as I did, there can be no doubt that we were far worse off for material choices than children today, yet in those days there was still a strong family code and a sense of community, both of which now seem to have largely vanished. The result is that, despite the proliferation of material goods, many more children than in previous generations are now suffering in the vitally important areas of moral and spiritual guidance, and consequently, as the result of an unstable family background, they are unable to make the most of their childhood (and possibly most important) years.

I suppose that a major factor in any child's enjoyment of life is that he or she is not expected to take on any of the weighty responsibilities which have to come later with adulthood. And so it was with me during the fifties, the time period covered by most of this book. I was relatively free, within the restraints quite rightly imposed by family and school, to do as I pleased with my spare time. Indeed boarding schools such as those I attended instilled in their pupils a sense of self-discipline; we were treated like adults their pupils a sense of self-discipline; we were treated like adults when we behaved like adults, but like small children if our behaviour warranted it. The use of the cane was a last resort but was generally effective.

In retrospect there can be no doubt that the world was somehow a simpler and more straightforward place to grow up in during the forties and fifties. People seemed more open and cooperative, perhaps because all families had needed to pull together during the war, frequently having to deal with the loss of the breadwinner, and now were enduring the many hardships that continued on for some years because of shortages of almost all material goods. But by the early fifties, and especially after the Festival of Britain Exhibition in 1951, there was a gradually growing acceptance that peace and stability were at last returning to this country, and that reasonable personal plans could be made without the fear of disruption. Parents then still considered it safe to allow children to go for long cycle rides alone, to play on the common, or to visit the cinema with their friends, things which few families would feel able to agree to today without a great deal of forethought. Those with children of their own will know what I mean.

Of course, to write an autobiography which wallows in nostalgia for its own sake is not necessarily very positive; it is obviously pointless to try to live in the past just because we may disapprove of the ways the world has changed so much in just a few decades. But if we can exercise control over our feelings, and keep them in their proper place, then looking back at events in our lives with a certain amount of objectivity enables us to recall places, people and events with a deep inner satisfaction. Even memories of the more difficult times of our childhood become more mellow with the passing of the years, and if we are honest with ourselves, didn't we have a great deal of fun as we grew up, even if we did lack all the 'sophisticated' entertainment that today's youngsters have at their fingertips?

So in this book I hope to be able recapture briefly the feelings of what it was like to grow up in the forties and fifties, with special reference to my interest in aviation, which started when I was still very young, as you will see.

We have a print in the hall at home which I have always liked; it depicts a child lying on the grass at the top of a cliff on a warm summer's day, and watching the seagulls as they wheel this way and that with seemingly effortless skill. I suppose that most of us have at some time done something similar; perhaps we have observed a flock of large water birds on a lake, and wondered at the natural control that they seem to have when landing and taking off, always doing so into the wind. I wonder how much they have to consciously think about what they are doing? Much of the procedure is probably 'hard-wired' into their brains, but even so they can still get it wrong sometimes!

The pioneers of flight must have envied the birds, wishing that they too could see the earth from above; now we all have the opportunity to fulfil this desire if we so wish, and perhaps seasoned travellers using the commercial airlines regularly may tend to take for granted the marvel of flight – unless they have some unpleasant experience to remind them that coming down is more natural than going up. As Spike Milligan has said: "Flying is absolutely safe: it's crashing that's dangerous!"

But to me, real flying has always meant sitting in a small cockpit, maybe an open one as in a Tiger Moth, and observing the countryside from just a thousand feet above; surely we cannot fail to be moved each time we see the ever-changing scenery unfolding beneath us. Even though we have spoiled so much of the earth's surface through wars, heavy industry, deforestation and unsympthetic agriculture, it is, as the late Louis Armstrong once put it so simply, "A Wonderful World," and Britain has its fair share of beauty still.

Being sent away to boarding school in Wales at the age of eight, and later to Lancing College in Sussex, I needed to develop very early on senses of both self-sufficiency and self-preservation, and these qualities certainly stood me in good stead as they enabled me to make the best of being away from home, to get on with people as well as I could and to develop leisure activities which could be enjoyed either with a companion or alone. This is why, with an already-existing interest in aircraft, it only needed a well-meaning nudge from my school friend Tim Foster in 1952 to start me off on the aeroplane-spotting hobby that has been a part of my life now for nearly fifty years. In particular my experiences at Shoreham Airport in the first half of the 1950s profoundly affected my life in my life in many ways.

But, one might ask quite reasonably, of what practical value is aeroplane-spotting? Don't we hear of young (and not so young) vandals breaking into hangars and causing wilful damage to aircraft? Isn't this the reason why a number of airfield owners are not too well disposed towards visitors by road? It is true that within the large band of aircraft enthusiasts, as well as in other leisure pursuits such as football, a mindless few can spoil everything for the conscientious majority, but that is no reason to stop everyone being aircraft enthusiasts or football supporters. With current pressures to close airfields or to severely restrict their movements, it seems to me that business and recreational aviation needs all the support it can get from genuine enthusiasts.

And after all, the information and photographs being recorded by enthusiasts now will be of much value to archivists in the future, just as what was current news in the fifties is very much a part of our history in the nineties. Was it really only those such as the founders of Air-Britain in 1948 who foresaw at that time the tremendous growth of interest in the history and development of aviation that is still occurring today amongst enthusiasts of all ages? I find it gratifying that, whenever I visit an aerodrome these days for a fly-in or some other aviation event, there are always many others present of my own age group or older, with just the same or even greater enthusiasm than mine. What a satisfying hobby it is, too, that you can continue pursuing whatever your age. And in addition, it is a healthy occupation: acres of green grass, fresh air, the breeze in your hair (or what is left of it!) and some gentle walking must be good for you – rather like golf, but without most of the frustrations! Our only occasional enemy is the British climate, which has attempted all sorts of ploys over the years intended to dampen our enthusiasm; I must confess that occasionally these have been only too successful.

Not everyone interested in aircraft has been able to obtain, and maintain, a Private Pilot's Licence. I was content just to be a passenger for quite some time, but eventually the urge to learn to fly began to get the better of me. I shall always recall the wonderful W.S. Shackleton Weekend at Sywell in 1962 when I had the opportunity to purchase an airworthy Taylorcraft Plus D for just £500. For some reason I did not, and have always regretted it. At the time I was still single and had a proportion of my income not allocated for the paying of bills and mortgages. In 1964 I finally took the plunge and joined the Three Counties Flying Club at Blackbushe during their first year of operations, completing about 9 hours of the PPL course, mostly in Linnet G-ASFW, at £5 per hour.

I then had to abandon any more lessons when I became engaged towards the end of the year and had to start saving for somewhere to live; I suspect that many others have been through the same scenario! Since then I have never been able to justify the expense of taking it up again.

From the late sixties until the late seventies my aviation activities receded into the background as I became more interested in classic cars, which were more accessible and presented opportunities for real hands-on experience of things mechanical. After I got married in 1965 I purchased a 1936 Austin Seven Ruby for £17 10s (the only time I have ever split a pound when buying a car!) and rebuilt it, and later when our son was born and we needed more space, I acquired a 1945 Austin 8, a car I had always liked. We used to attend quite a lot of rallies up and down the country in the late sixties and seventies. Occasionally they coincided with an aircraft meeting; I remember one at Slinfold, Sussex, in 1971, and another at Newbury Racecourse in 1978. In fact it was in that year that my partly-dormant interest in aircraft was reawakened, and from then on I began to attend the annual PFA Rally and other flying meetings.

It was late in 1989, during a particularly depressing wet winter's weekend, that I started to wonder if there were other people just like me who would like to be able to look back with affection to the fifties and what we aircraft enthusiasts got up to then. It was these thoughts that encouraged me to tackle the writing of this particular book. I have needed to search out and dust off my diaries right back to the forties when I was first sent away to school; I have also had to go carefully through such classic books as Ian Allan's *"Civil Aircraft Markings 1953"* and countless odd scraps of paper preserved with care over the intervening years, and try to put all the information in some sort of order so that it will mean something to the reader.

So I hope that you will derive as much pleasure out of reading the narrative and browsing through the Appendices as I have had in putting all the information together. The first edition, which was published in 1990 as a rather amateur effort, was sufficiently well received to make me realise that it would be worth doing an enlarged version and get it printed professionally. These copies have now also been sold, and this modest success has provided me with a good excuse to prepare an extended edition.

Hopefully there is enough of general interest in the main text to satisfy the criteria for a 'good read,' even if you are not as hooked on aeroplanes as I am! In my experience as a book publisher in recent years, I have found that there are those of us who love to have a valid reason to dig out their records from years long past, either to compare notes with what an author has written, or in some cases with the intention of putting together their own personal story. There must still be hundreds of volumes out there just waiting to be written, and I am glad that we have been able to publish some of them in our recent trilogy about flying in the fifties.

May I finally add a word of caution? Do please bear in mind that, as in any work of this sort, there are likely to be errors and omissions in the recorded aircraft data; I would be very pleased to hear from any readers with their comments, especially if they have discovered something amiss that can be put right if there is a further reprint, or if they can throw any light on some of the missing details.

In addition to the material published here, I have a great deal more that is not specifially mentioned. For example, I still have details of the aircraft I logged at every aerodrome visit I have ever made from 1952 onwards, although some is probably well-documented elsewhere. Please feel free to get in touch with me in your search for historical information, or if you are considering publication of your own personal archive material; I'll certainly do my best to help you!

Peter Campbell

CHAPTER 1
WARTIME MEMORIES

My father, Harold Gordon Campbell (he always hated the Harold and so was always known as Gordon) was a qualified electrical and mechanical engineer with a degree from King's College, London. Before the war he worked on contracts in Scotland for power companies which aimed to provide a mains electricity supply to the remoter parts of the Highlands. His father, the head teacher at Windsor Park School in Musselburgh, just outside Edinburgh, had been born on Shapinsay (one of the Orkney Isles), he was born in Edinburgh, and I was born in Woking!

Before she married, my mother Violet had had two careers. She had been a fairly well-known sportswoman, playing hockey for England and tennis for Surrey, and she was also an opera singer. My father had admired her for some years before he got up the courage to propose – they were both well over forty when they were married in 1936. I was born some nine months later in June 1937.

In 1941, when I was three years and nine months old, my mother started sending me to a local infants' school in Woking, St. Benet's, which was within walking distance of our home. Apparently I could already read (a tribute to the teaching skill that my mother obviously must have had – it's never too early for children to start learning) and soon I was learning arithmetic, which I also thoroughly enjoyed. Other subjects can't have been so riveting, as I began to doze off one day whilst sitting on a window ledge, leant back and broke the window; fortunately I didn't fall out. Later I learned that I was going to need to wear glasses for the rest of my life, but this didn't really seem a problem then, and seldom has been since, except for playing school games such as football and cricket.

I find it hard to understand even now that, as my mother much later admitted to me, she had not wanted to reveal to me that there was a war on! Perhaps, using her maternal instincts, she had had my best interests at heart, but once I was at school with the children of other families the war became a very real experience. However, we had never really known anything different.

My father, who was well into his fifties by this time, was frequently away working for the Admiralty in Bath, so my mother arranged to take in an 'evacuee' from London (someone with an interest in music was specified), and in March 1940 a teenage girl called Joyce Honner arrived; she stayed with us for two and a half years, and I still keep in touch with her now – she was like an older sister to me. We developed a routine for when the air raid sirens went off in the middle of the night; we hastily put on some warm clothes over our nightwear and cautiously made our way down the garden to the relative safety of the Anderson air raid shelter, in which we spent a few hours in some sort of cold comfort. However, sometimes we had to spend the entire night in there, which was a lot more daunting; being underground we had to get used to such inconveniences as having columns of ants crossing the bed! But our home in Woking was some twenty-five miles from the centre of London and we never suffered any serious bomb damage locally.

My first recollection of anything to do with aeroplanes is from sometime near the end of the war, probably late in 1944 when I was just seven years old. However the event that occurred on this particular late summer day is firmly etched in my conscious mind and reveals that even before then I must taken more than a passing interest in aircraft recognition.

We were visiting my grandmother that afternoon; she lived only about ten minutes' walk away in a fine Victorian family home, Loxley House, with a garden of about an acre or so. Here I'm compelled to digress yet again for a moment, as I discovered fairly recently that this particular house can be identified in H.G. Wells' book *"The War of the Worlds."* At the time when he wrote it he was living in digs in Maybury Road, Woking, alongside the main railway line to London, and the Martian invasion was supposed to have taken place in the sandpits on Horsell Common, just a mile or so to the north, and just south of what is now Fairoaks Airport. H.G. Wells described the events in detail such as would only have been available to someone who knew the area well, and there is no doubt that in his imagination my grandmother's house played a significant part in the story.

But back to the Loxley House garden! Fresh fruit straight from the apple and peach trees was a real luxury in those days of food rationing and general shortages, and on this particular occasion my mother and I were enjoying the sunshine and a freshly picked apple when the quiet was disturbed by a strange whining noise in the sky, which proved to be a 'doodlebug' coming in our direction and not very high up. Suddenly there was a sound of gunfire, followed by the throaty roar of a Merlin engine, and a Spitfire (with clipped wings, I remember) did a victory roll overhead; I can still see clearly the silver wings with their large Royal Air Force roundels glinting in the sunlight. However, my mother, not in any way convinced that the danger was past, and obviously believing that the aircraft was bent on attacking us, shouted at me to take cover and started to drag me towards the tall hedge which surrounded the garden. Not being very well matched for size (she was almost six feet tall), I didn't find it easy to convince her that the plane was one of ours! We later heard that the 'doodlebug' had indeed been shot down (or tipped over?) by the Spitfire and had crashed in a market garden about two miles away, fortunately with no casualties.

I also recall that on another occasion a young fighter pilot who lived in a house at the foot of the hill nearby decided, despite previous official warnings, to show off his skills to his family once again and indulged in some extra-low flying that could have so easily ended in tragedy; the plane came seemingly straight at our house and can have cleared it with only feet to spare.

Towards the end of the war my mother took me for a break to South Shields, the home of my father's sister, Bessie Campbell. This overlooked the park and I can recall winding up my toy Minic clockwork lorries and letting them run along the paths, which for some reason always attracted other children – surely they had seen Minic and Dinky toys up there?

Such were the memories, some significant and some not, that imprinted themselves on young minds in those days; we were too young to understand the real horrors of war, and that some 55 million lives had been sacrificed by the time the B-29 "Enola Gay" dropped the first atom bomb on Hiroshima. Contrary to expectations, very little seems to have changed for the better since then in any lasting way; why is it that whenever we invent something which has enormous potential for good, we seem to focus all our efforts into developing it so that we can kill one another more efficiently and expensively? Such thoughts obviously must have gone through the mind of the pilot of "Enola Gay," who is reported as having a guilty conscience for the rest of his life with the recurring vision of the incalculable suffering he had indirectly caused; however the rear gunner is reported not to have been affected in that way – perhaps to him it was "just another job."

We all had to come to terms with the realities of life, however, as we grew up, and although I continued to be fascinated by anything that flew I decided to focus my main attention on smaller civil aircraft; apart from their being more accessible, they hadn't been designed to be used for killing people. It concerns me somewhat that, more than fifty years on, there still seems to be such a nostalgic yearning in the minds of some for a return to the 'spirit,' if not the reality, of wartime; there are countless museums, societies and preservation groups only too proud to show off their aircraft, guns, tanks and military vehicles, and indeed many aircraft owners decorate their mounts with full wartime paint schemes and markings. The common argument in favour of this practice is of course 'realism,' which I can understand up to a point; but do we really want to prolong the memories of war? Can we honestly say that we have ever learned from our previous mistakes? Despite the undoubted cameraderie that existed, no one could legitimately claim that war is the best time for making new friends and enjoying oneself. Is it really so then, as I have heard some people say, that what we need is another war to encourage this country to pull itself together, or to solve the overpopulation problems of the world? All very well maybe in theory, unless you happen to be one of the victims. But that is quite enough of moralising!

I have just a few rather vague and generalised impressions of the next few months. I can certainly remember hearing on the radio the news that the war had come to an end, the announcement of VJ-Day, eating my first ice-cream, being offered my first banana ("What on earth is that?") and then the news was broken to me by my parents that I was to be sent off to boarding school. They later told me that this was because they believed that as an only child I would have a much better time there both socially and educationally, and there is no doubt that it was a great financial sacrifice for them. Whether their aims were justified I cannot tell, as you can't run control experiments with your children.

But, in retrospect, things can't have been too bad after that: after all, I'm still here!

CHAPTER 2
COTTESMORE DAYS
(1945-1951)

It was towards the end of the war that I came to know two boys who later became good friends, John Green and David Timmis; they lived close by, and coincidentally had been born on the same day in 1938; I was just over a year older.

We enjoyed several years of racing up and down the lane on our bikes, playing studiously with model railways (at first O-gauge clockwork and then Hornby Dublo) and flying gliders on some spare land across the road which belonged to a block of flats called Maybury House; often we were shooed away by the bad-tempered old caretaker, whom we nicknamed "Grizzly Grumps."

After the war the Timmis family moved across town to Horsell; their new house had a long drive, a grass tennis court, an enormous greenhouse (which in season was always full of succulent grapes) and a couple of acres of garden. I was always made a welcome visitor and spent many happy days there during the holidays before being sent off back to boarding school.

During the late forties and early fifties David and I became reasonably proficient with model aeroplanes, both rubber-powered and gliders. We also developed our speciality line of small high-speed solid balsa models; these were launched off a catapult powered by more than a yard of thick elastic, the catapult being attached to a five-foot wooden post driven into the ground of Wheatsheaf Common. These models were fairly simple to build but were to futuristic designs (usually in swept-wing or delta configurations), and had a wing span of not more than a foot or so.

To prepare for flight, the rubber was attached to a projecting pin secured in the underside of the fuselage; the model was then pulled back to stretch the elastic as far as we dared, and then we let go. The plane would leave our hand so fast that we could not follow its progress with the naked eye, until after a few seconds we could see it coming out of an enormous loop and bearing down on us from behind. It was indeed very spectacular, and even more so if we had not set the trim right – there was then a pile of matchwood to collect.

The school chosen for the dubious honour of caring for my betterment was Cottesmore. It was founded in 1894 by a Colonel Davison-Brown, and was given that name as a memorial to his fiancée who had been killed in a hunting accident with the Cottesmore Hunt. The school had been based in Hove, Sussex, prior to the second World War, but for reasons of safety had been moved to North Wales in 1940 for the duration of the hostilities. The Oakeley Arms Hotel at Tan-y-Bwlch had been a peaceful temporary resting place, but after a short stay more suitable accomodation became available.

This was Cors-y-Gedol Hall, near Barmouth, a former Charles I hunting lodge, and was described by Michael Rogerson, the headmaster, in the school magazine for 1940:

"Let us now try to describe this place which is to become a part of us. If you catch the 9.10 am train from Paddington you arrive at Barmouth at 4 o'clock. If our petrol coupons have run out you will have to take a bus or taxi and travel for four miles along the Harlech road. At Dyffryn appear the entrance gates guarded by two lodges. After a journey up the mile-long drive which climbs 500 feet in a dead straight line, you catch the first glimpses of the Hall through an avenue of trees. You will have done the same as Charles I when he ran from Cromwell in 1642. The same old cedar tree will be there but instead of the cries of ostlers you will hear the shouts of boys. Cors-y-Gedol has a history, it has already been rejuvenated in form and now it will be in spirit.

There are large airy rooms with beautiful panelling, modern conveniences have been installed, and the walls that have weathered centuries give ample warmth and protection against the Welsh weather. Behind on the east rises Moelfre, 2,000 feet high; woods form a protection against the westerly winds. There is a two-acre kitchen garden with one of those walls of which one dreams. The farm is attached – a farm consisting of 3,000 acres (we shall at least be sure of our butter!). There are lakes in which fish can be caught. There are playing fields and they are flat.

We sincerely hope that one day soon you will be able to escape the bombs and catch that 9.10 train from Paddington."

Michael has also recalled in his autobiography "In and out of School" that the water and electricity supplies depended on a stream, which often froze or got blocked up with dead sheep.

Thus it was that one September day in 1945 this eight-year-old found himself sitting in that very train pulling out of Paddington at 9.10 am, along with dozens of other small boys of varying shapes, sizes and degrees of cleanliness. I was only in Wales for one term before we moved back to Sussex but I remember that at first I disliked fervently the loneliness of it all; after all, I had never before been away from my parents for more than a day. I used to gaze longingly at the aircraft as they climbed out of Llanbedr airfield a few miles away, wishing that one of them would take me home.

But I soon found plenty of things to do to pass my spare time; one of my favourite pastimes was collecting an enormous variety of empty cartridge and shell cases that the military had left behind on the slopes of Moelfre. The woods nearby also provided adventure, with rival gangs of small dishevelled boys tracking each other down and taking 'prisoners' until teatime.

Returning to the area now, it all looks much the same as it was then, apart from the proliferation of caravan sites. The woods and lake and the cedar tree are still there at the Hall, only now 'Bed & Breakfast' is on offer. About fifteen years ago when I returned to the area on holiday for the first time since the war, I met, quite by chance, the baker who used to make and deliver our bread all those long years ago!

Early in 1946 the school moved back to its original prewar premises in Hove, Sussex. Michael Rogerson had been looking for a postwar location for the expanding school which would be more suitable than the previous premises at Hove, which had had the Army billeted in them. He had decided on Buchan Hill, near the village of Pease Pottage, just off the main London-to-Brighton road. Unfortunately things didn't quite work out timewise, and it was necessary for the school to return to Hove for two terms before Buchan Hill became available.

I can't remember very much about Hove except that there was an outdoor swimming pool, complete with changing rooms in an old wheel-less railway carriage from the Victorian era.

During the term prior to the move to Buchan Hill, all of us were taken by bus to have a look round the new site, a country mansion with many acres of land suitable for playing fields, woods for exploring and a lake for swimming in. Unbeknown to us, the headmaster's brother-in-law, Dudley Farmer (who used to visit the school quite regularly once we had moved to Buchan Hill and who we all used to think was the spitting image of King George VI), was scheduled to give us quite a surprise. We were all relaxing in the grounds after lunch when the headmaster announced that he had forgotten to bring any sweets with him. These valuable commodities were of course essential fare at any picnic, and loud groans emanated from all and sundry.

"Never mind," he said, "I've asked the Air Ministry to send a plane over with some."

We showed our disbelief in typical manner.

But imagine how we felt when, shortly after this, an aeroplane did indeed appear, flying very low and slow with flaps down, and proceeded to deposit three large bags of sweets about fifty yards away from us on the large flat area that would later become the playing fields. The ensuing commotion was my first introduction to unofficial rugby scrums and not a few heads were bruised, but fortunately there were plenty of sweets for everyone! In hindsight, remembering that all confectionery must have been in very short supply just after the war, quite a few adults must have given up their rations for some time in order to provide us, the starving masses, with such an special treat.

A review of the day appeared in the next issue of the school magazine, "*The Cottesmorian.*"

"*On Monday July 8th . . . directly after chapel we all changed and after a short spell in the cricket field we embussed – together with much food – for our journey to Buchan Hill where we were going to inspect our new home. The weather was glorious and we departed from Hove in high spirits. On our arrival at Buchan Hill we divided up into Sets and Mr Rogerson and Mr Moll conducted us over the House and Grounds respectively. Then followed a grand picnic lunch, the most notable feature of which was the efforts of some boys to consume jelly – which had been doled out to them in cups – without spoons. Apparently only one thing had been forgotten – SWEETS! But in the middle of the afternoon, when we were taking a well-earned rest in the shade of some trees, an aeroplane suddenly flew across the ground and launched some missiles at us. All was well, however, for these objects, which the more timid of us had taken to be bombs, turned out to be bags of sweets. There was at once a general stampede and one bag was captured intact. The other two bags burst on landing and for the rest of the afternoon boys could be observed searching the long grass on their hands and knees in a manner reminiscent of an earnest bug-hunter on the trail of some rare specimen.*"

I have always been able to recall this incident as clearly as if it happened yesterday. About ten years ago, in an attempt to try and find out a little more about the exercise, I wrote to the retired headmaster Michael Rogerson (now regrettably deceased – his son Mark carries on the family tradition) to see if he could enlighten me. In due course I had a most interesting letter in reply from his wife Marion, which contained an extract from a letter written by the pilot himself, Dudley Farmer, to his sister saying the following:

"The flight was put down as 'local flying' as it was against King's Regulations to drop sweets to boys from His Majesty's aircraft! It was worth risking a Court Martial because of all the kindness you both have always shown me."

Despite some other information in that letter, and some more recent research, I have as yet failed to identify with any certainty the actual aircraft involved. What I do know is that it was an Auster, was fairly new, was based at Gatwick, and had the call sign '544.' As I am certain that it was painted silver, it must presumably have been a Mk. 5 and not one of the new Mk. 6s as I believe that the latter were finished in camouflage; perhaps it could have been TJ544, which, I gather, had recently been in Germany – I will probably never know for sure. The RAF Museum at Hendon tell me that at the time there were two communications flights at Gatwick, 85 Group Communications Squadron and a detachment from 84 Group, but that both moved out in August 1946. So that July things must have already been winding down. An inconsequential mystery really, but one I would still like to get to the bottom of.

So in the autumn of 1946 we relocated once again. Buchan Hill had been used during the war by the Pearl Assurance Company as their Fire Department, but it was now surplus to their requirements. It had originally been built in about 1880 in a Jacobean-cum-Victorian style, and the story behind it is quite fascinating.

During much of the Victorian period, ostrich feathers were very fashionable for decoration on ladies' clothing and hats, and a Mr Saillard, who farmed ostriches in South Africa, had built up a very successful business. Then in the late 1870s fashions changed, the business suffered a severe decline and, to cap it all, one of Mr Saillard's ostriches died suddenly. He was determined to pin down the cause of death, which perhaps he felt was a bad omen, and discovered that the bird had a diamond stuck in its throat. On the principle "always try to turn adversity to your advantage" (which still holds just as good today), he managed to discover the source of the diamond, found that there were plenty more where that one had come from, and quickly was able to amass a large fortune. He then returned to the UK and had Buchan Hill built as a family home.

None of us will ever forget the bitterly cold and prolonged winter of 1946-1947, but as children we revelled in the snow and ice, particularly when the sun shone all day as it did for part of March. The usual routine of games was disrupted, but there were plenty of other childish pursuits to follow outside: these included chasing each other around and through the zareba (a large enclosure mainly comprising evergreen shrubs), snowballing, tobogganing, sucking enormous icicles broken off a wire fence, and running onto the frozen lake to try and slide as far across as we could.

I can remember seeing my first DC-3 in 1947, and being puzzled at the apparently asymmetric (although illusory) configuration of the engines. And, being familiar with the Dragon Rapide, I was puzzled to see one flying over which had four engines instead of two; at the time I was not aware of the existence of the DH.86 Express – this one was probably G-ADUH or G-ADVJ belonging to Bond Air Services of Gatwick.

Outside our schoolwork times, there were all sorts of recreational opportunities, and we were encouraged to develop useful skills and hobbies. Apart from practising the piano, I spent a lot of time in the excellent 0-gauge model railway room in the basement, and I also designed, made and flew a variety of model aeroplanes along with the school expert, John Peters. (The last I heard was that John was now a Lord and something big in the Department of the Environment.) Other facilities available in the huge cellars must have been quite unusual for the time: they included a shooting range, ten-pin bowling, carpentry, photography, Meccano, printing and pottery.

Another unusual facility for those times was a three-quarter-size billiards table, which amazingly has survived many generations of small boys still to be used today; doubtless it has been recovered many times – and no, I don't mean from the bottom of the lake. It was at this table that I was first introduced to billiards, snooker, and the newly-invented game of 'slosh.' Other 'upstairs' facilities included stamp clubs, chess, bridge, table tennis and art.

Two features of school life I thoroughly detested. One was boxing: even at the young age of ten I could see no point whatsoever in trying to knock the living daylights out of one's schoolmates, and I used to have long impassioned arguments with the teacher, Gerry Moll: as I recall, he eventually conceded to my impassioned view and I was excused. The other was the dreaded school play: this was an annual exercise guaranteed to make most of us squirm with embarrassment if we were actually in the play (and especially if we had drawn the shortest straw of all and were cast in a female role, as I was once when someone was needed who could play the piano); if we were part of the audience the general aim was to heckle our schoolmates throughout in an attempt –

often successful – to make them forget what they were meant to say and do next.

Outside was another world entirely. The grounds were extensive, and gave plenty of opportunities for exploration, while the lake was also extensive and gave plenty of opportunities for getting wet. But before we were ever allowed in the lake we had to be painstakingly taught the basics of swimming in the "Duck Pond," a more traditional outdoor pool; this I mastered eventually, but only after a lot of special tuition. To encourage those who found it difficult, a piece of kit had been designed that basically comprised a pole with a piece of rope hanging from one end and a loop of heavy-duty webbing at the end of it, which went around your torso. Thus supported, you could practise the strokes in the water in the reassurance that the sports master would not let you go under if you were not as buoyant as you hoped. Once 'passed out,' I revelled in the opportunities to swim in the lake; there was a large raft some way out, so there was something to aim for and to rest on for a while, and when races were held, the raft was of course the turning point.

But I was never really a sporting type. For a start I wore glasses, which precluded my being proficient at most games, as I was unable to see clearly enough without them. I was left-handed and left-footed, although by some quirk played a right-handed game when I needed to use *both* hands – such as when batting at cricket or playing golf. Cricket was the most difficult for me without my glasses; the ball was small and of course there were no such things as protection helmets in those days. My batting innings would usually last for no longer than three balls: the first delivery I would flail at wildly and miss completely, the second I would somehow connect with and score a boundary four, and on the third I would be either bowled out or caught. My prowess as a left-handed bowler was more recognised as I developed a cunning technique to produce a vicious off-spin on the ball, which sometimes I used and sometimes I didn't. . . .

Soccer and rugby were not quite so difficult for me as the ball was larger. I played left back (and sometimes outside left) at soccer and again developed a cunning strategy of kicking the ball from a *right-hand* corner so that it curved right into the net (sometimes). Because of my build I was considered useful as ballast in rugby scrums (as a second-row forward, when my ears were always sore afterwards); but I was never very effective, except in place-kicking, which I did my best to develop to a fine art. Amazingly I was awarded my school colours. My motto on the sports field perhaps should have been "More by guile than by talent."

Neither were athletics a strong point; regular cross-country running was encouraged, but I didn't have the stamina, and my only triumph was winning a silver spoon as second prize in the long jump in 1949 (12 ft 3 in). At least it made a change from the more usual: "You're for the high jump."

For our more leisurely moments we were also encouraged to have our own garden plots (about 8 ft by 3 ft), and we grew more or less whatever we fancied, but mainly quick-growing annuals and seldom anything edible.

Occasionally on fine summer days the whole school had an informal picnic in the woods; fried sausages garnished with miscellaneous pieces of twig and bracken had an appeal all of their own and these events were very popular with everyone. Of course we were all fond of sausages, as are children of all generations. With meat strictly rationed, it was usual for sausages to be padded out with things like breadcrumbs, soya flour and milk powder, and there is an apocryphal story of the times told about an MP who asked in the House: "How much milk powder is permitted to be put in a sausage before it becomes legally a cream bun?" In those early postwar days it was certainly difficult to make both ends meat.

Our school milk came in 1/3-pint bottles with its own built-in entertainment. The lid was a cardboard disc, and one of these, with a notch cut in it, proved a excellent projectile for propulsion by a rubber band, potentially quite lethal although some protection was afforded if you wore glasses. We used to run competitions for accuracy.

Some of the more unpleasant memories of boarding school are also associated in my mind with food. Imagine the problem of catering for some eighty children soon after the war, yet really we had little reason to complain. Although tinned sweet corn was intended to be a treat, I could never accept the taste, and won't eat sweet corn or corn on the cob to this day! But two legitimate (to my mind) moans were the potatoes, sometimes containing cooked grubs, and the meat, much of which seemed to be gristle and fat. School rules dictated that we cleared our plates, and consequently we had to resort to devious tactics to overcome the problem, such as hiding bits in our handkerchieves, or purposely dropping pieces on the floor out of sight (as we thought). I just couldn't swallow gristle or fat, and I remember spending much of one weekend in disgrace and confined to bed because of my misdemeanours.

A common punishment inflicted on minor miscreants (i.e. those undeserving of the cane or being sent to bed) was "facing the paint." The book compiled recently by the present headmaster, Mark Rogerson, entitled *One Hundred Years of Cottesmore – An Anthology: 1894–1994,"* quotes extracts of essays from pupils and their thoughts on this form of punishment:

"'Facing the paint' . . . consists of standing up against a wall with your face towards it, quite still and silent. Now here [at Buchan Hill] we are usually meant to face the paint outside Mr Hilder's study, but at Cors-y-Gedol [Wales] I knew what the paint looked like in every spot of the house, and am beginning to know part of it here – as I did in Hove too. At Cors-y-Gedol I began to resort to other things than just looking at it. I began to eat it. This may sound silly at first, but the plaster in the playroom was easily detachable, and I entertained a vague sort of hope that when all the paint was eaten I'd have none to face."

"The recognised method of trying to get sympathy is by giving a hollow churchyard cough every now and then (this can easily be brought to perfection after a little practice). . . . To attract the attention of the master or monitor who put you there, so that he will see how well you are behaving, give a short cough, or even clear your throat, and stand with your hands behind your back without moving a muscle. However, if he does appear to notice, it would be best to relax, as there is no need to have your sinews aching for nothing. If you are in the classroom, an entertaining but somewhat dangerous way of passing the time is to try and edge round the room back to where you started from without being seen. I must, however, emphasize the peril of such manoeuvres. And if you aren't daring enough to try and amuse yourself, you can at least, after a little practice, go to sleep on your feet."

There was a very individualistic team of teachers at Cottesmore. I particularly liked Gerry Moll (English & Sports), who lived near Woking and occasionally provided transport for me in his Morris Eight at the beginnings and ends of terms, and Peter Crawford (Maths). Alan Hilder (History) was held in awe by many of us as he could have quite a fearsome demeanour and was not averse to aiming a blackboard cleaner (a wooden block faced with felt) at you during class; perhaps this is the reason I never got on well with History as a subject. Yet it was in his study that I and others were entertained from time to time, and where I first heard such classic records as Nöel Coward's "Mad Dogs and Englishmen" and "The Stately Homes of England," and Fred Astaire and Judy

Garland's rendering of "We're a Couple of Swells" from the film "Easter Parade." For some reason he also encouraged me to learn Greek: this I did and the basic knowledge I gained has come in very useful over the years, especially in the publishing business where correct spelling – and hence some knowledge of etymology – is essential.

Our Matron was Nurse Oakden, although we just knew her as "Nurse." She was a 'tyrant' in the nicest possible way. She stood for absolutely no nonsense, yet she was always there when needed, and apparently never had a day's illness herself all through her many years at the school. She called most boys "Toeface" although my particular nickname was "Cambodia." I can see her now, striding along the corridors with her starched white headdress bouncing up and down with each step.

I have other memories of those times which will ring a bell with anyone of a similar age to myself. The immediate postwar years produced a number of new inventions which were made available to the public. If nothing else, the war had expedited the development of all sorts of technologies, and some of the spin-offs from that era have eventually benefitted us all.

My father took advantage of them all. He was an engineer, inveterate golfer and part-time inventor himself, and being of Scottish extraction he hated waste (Scots are not mean, just careful), and designed what I believe was one of the first devices for retrieving golf balls from the bottoms of ponds; this comprised three metal shafts that fitted inside another with a three-pronged stainless steel 'grabber' on the end. During trials by the pond at the local golf course, we discovered that no golf ball in less about ten feet of water was safe, but then neither was I as I squatted precariously by the edge.

He was also fascinated by other new commercial products, and introduced me to the wonders of Sellotape. My popularity at school soared rapidly when I became the proud possessor of what appeared to be the only roll in the place: however it plummeted just as rapidly when I refused to allow anyone to have more than about two inches at a time, and I soon became well-known for my Scottish ancestry.

At more or less the same time (in 1948) I was introduced in an oblique way to a very famous name in aviation, that of Miles. With hindsight it is perhaps ironic that this introduction should have occurred at much the same time that the aircraft company, which had enjoyed so much success before, during and after the war, was folding up.

An unexpected gift from my father was one of the very first ballpoint pens, introduced as the Miles Biro pen. In those days they cost fifty-five shillings each (£2.75 in today's money), an enormous sum when you consider that a large loaf of bread then cost only about sixpence (2½p). Now, of course, you can buy a ballpoint pen for about 20p and a loaf costs about five times as much! Despite the fact that the writing tended to smudge in time as the oil in the ink spread slowly through the paper, nevertheless it was a tremendous advance technically. Today we have ceased to wonder at such things as Sellotape and ballpoint pens, but at that time they were genuine breakthoughs with positive benefits for all. I can't help wondering if there are any other relatively simple aids to living still to be discovered. Most new gadgets are nowadays described by marketing experts as 'sophisticated' in the sense that all civilised people need one whether they realise it or not, and to my mind they are indeed sophisticated, but in the true sense of the word, as any good dictionary will tell you ("unnecessarily complicated").

At the end of each term, the examinations were held. After we had had our marked papers returned, it was up to us to do the necessary research to correct all our mistakes. We then had to wait to see each teacher in turn and present our efforts to him to be verified. We took with us what we used to call our "Passport to Freedom." On this document (made by the pupils individually) we not only recorded the number of hours left until the official end of term, which we crossed off religiously: we had allocated space on special pages to record the signature of each master once he was satisfied that our corrections were to his liking. When all the necessary signatures had been acquired, we waited for the right moment to approach the Headmaster; then once we had his signature too, we were free from doing any more work until the end of term. You can imagine the high spirits that prevailed from then on amongst those freed from 'slave labour,' and the frustrations of those less fortunate pupils still beavering away whilst their colleagues whooped it up.

At the risk of being accused of name-dropping, we boys from ordinary backgrounds had the opportunity to mix with the sons of several famous parents; these included Tarquin, the son of Sir Laurence Olivier and Vivien Leigh, the two sons of the author Alun Williams (one was Brook, who became an actor, and enters the story again later – the name of the other escapes me, regretfully) and Lance Callingham, the son of Sir Bernard and Lady Docker. Mind you, although the parents may have been famous, that didn't mean much to us at that age really; boys will be boys, and one youngster looks, speaks and behaves much like another, especially when liberally covered with mud during a game of football.

From time to time we were given film shows and other entertainments, and at the end of the Christmas term there was the Feast to look forward to; this was first instituted in 1946, shortly after our move to Buchan Hill and, considering the constraints of these times just after the war, it is truly amazing what the headmaster and his wife were able to organise. Apart from the meal itself there were candles, holly, crackers and – best of all – dishes of sweets. Rules were relaxed so much that we were allowed to have as many helpings of pudding (mince pies, Christmas Pudding, fruit salad, jelly and trifle) as we could manage. We were then entertained by various members of staff while we allowed our digestive systems to take a well-earned rest.

A special occasion during our last year before leaving was to be invited in small groups to the Headmaster's study (a place that was never normally entered voluntarily) for a social evening. (We also had individual sessions about the 'facts of life'.) The Headmaster and his wife had a television set, and they were kind enough to allow us to sample what was on offer; it was there that I first saw the Beverley Sisters as long ago as 1950.

At this point I must mention the potato saga. In those hard times it seemed sensible to the powers-that-were to supplement potato supplies by growing some to help feed the school. In the spring of 1950 several tons of seed potatoes were planted in a large field belonging to a local farmer, with the aid of 'slave labour,' i.e. us. By the autumn, despite all sorts of difficulties due to blight, bad weather and various agricultural problems, the potatoes were ready for lifting, and again many of us were volunteered to help collect them. Reading again the Cottesmore Centenary book has reminded me of the details of this episode, and I am grateful to be able to now quote part of an article that appeared in the school magazine:

"The boys returned to School at the end of September and the farmer was informed in good time that labour was plentiful and willing (to get off Latin). Could he possibly please produce his implements and we could have the job done in a couple of days or even less? No, work on the farm had been held up with wet weather and the fine spell was just what he wanted to catch up. The spuds must wait and of course we understood this, but it worried us to see the days go by with those spuds still underground.

At last, however, a day was fixed. A Monday in mid-October – 9 o'clock – all the labour he wanted. Down came the rain. Classes as usual after all. But it cleared up when we had our noses in Latin grammar and the farmer went away in a huff. We eventually made it up and did get started. The machine, which resembled one of those mine-flailing tanks, was very old, and the driver of the tractor had never handled it before. It broke down. We were then informed that the job was impossible with bracken so high. We got up some spuds but at least twenty-five per cent escaped us. Then the farmer really did desert us. I think he thought we were mad. We also had some thoughts about him! But we cut down the bracken.

After a week or so we tentatively got on the phone and asked if he would let someone else use his infernal machine. He of course was only too glad.

We started again. 8 am the new man came; 9, labour available; 10, shear broken and taken to forge; 11.15, resume work; 12.15, driver off for dinner; 1.15, driver returns but labour off for dinner; 2.15, resume work; 3.15, shear broken and taken to forge – work stops. Total day's operation – three hours.

And so it went on. We never had more than one hour's consecutive work. It rained. We used an old horse potato plough. It broke. We got another. That broke, but we finished in a blaze of glory with the old infernal machine, bent and battered but still turning on November 7th. Total hours operating, twelve, spread over four weeks (total hours reckoned by our farmers, thirty-seven at 10s 6d an hour). A passer-by remarked: "Serves you right, them spuds should have been out a month ago." Never mind, we had won eighteen tons for three tons and there will be enough in the ground to have a good crop next year – but I'm not getting them out!"

I remember being part of the collecting team who picked up the potatoes and put them into large hessian sacks. It would have been backbreaking work for an adult, but as we were somewhat shorter we kept going quite well. It was certainly better than doing Latin grammar. There was another compensation, too: we all got paid pocket-money for our efforts.

In 1951 we were taken *en masse* to the official opening of Crawley New Town by Princess Elizabeth. We were herded together at the corner of a road junction at which HRH would alight from the royal car and perform the opening ceremony. The local paper recorded the event, of course, and there in next week's issue was the ugly mug of yours truly clearly visible (amongst about eighty others) and grinning inanely.

In *"One Hundred Years of Cottesmore"* a short piece is included which was apparently written by myself when the time came for me to leave Cottesmore in 1951. I am flattered that it was thought to be of sufficient literary merit to be dug out once again after being filed away for all that time. I reproduce it here for what it's worth.

"I am among the few boys now in the school who remember Wales very well – and I shall never forget the fun we used to have in the woods below Cors-y-Gedol Hall. There used to be two gangs: one the Jungle Patrol, the other the Black Gang, which consisted mainly of monitors, so gaining the inappropriate nickname "Baby Gang."

A small stream flowed out of the woods; we used to dam it with earth or mud, and Clement-Davies built a miniature 'city' on its banks. Then there was an enormous uprooted tree, commonly known as "HMS Baldeggs," though I cannot think why. We used to climb its massive roots and have mock battles. (Everyone thought of battles, as it was wartime.) I remember once when I was lost in the 'Jungle.' I tried many times to find my way out, but in vain; so I sat down and ate elderberries – there was an abundance of them everywhere – and these so refreshed me that I was able to find my way out almost at once.

Then we went to Hove: I remember the monotonous walks in the park; the swimming pool, and the railway coach without wheels in which we used to undress; and the day when we burned the third-game field almost bare of its grass. And I remember the lecture on "Ze Mazionettes" (Marionettes)! [A hilarious talk on puppets given by a Frenchman with little command of English]. *I don't know why, but I was violently sick afterwards! Then, as Hove was so battered by tanks and planes, we moved to Buchan Hill – nearly five years ago.*

I shall always remember the carved wooden faces in the schoolroom here. At the end of an English period, Williams I suddenly burst out laughing; on enquiring what the matter could be, we discovered that he was laughing at these faces. One of them, he said, looked like his brother.

I shall always remember all the masters from whom I have learnt. Counting them on my fingers I can bring to mind thirty-three who were with us at different times. They are people to whom I owe a great deal.

And so at the end of this term I leave Cottesmore with all its friendly faces, and go to a 'new world' at Lancing, where I only know a few boys and one master.

But I am determined to enjoy myself!"

And so I did in many ways, as will become apparent later on.

I can remember a few other events from the latter half of the forties which were unconnected with school, such as my father driving me down to Wittering on the Sussex coast on the 7th September 1946 to witness the successful world air speed record attempt by Gp. Capt. Donaldson in the Meteor 4 EE549.

More sport-orientated excursions included a day at the 1948 Olympic Games at Wembley with Joyce Honner, and my first visit to Twickenham for a Rugby International match with John Green and his parents.

I also was invited to a party at the home of my schoolfriend John Peters, and was taken to one side by the conjurer and asked to be his accomplice. I had a 'pretend' dead chicken stuffed down my shorts (which was produced with aplomb at the appropriate moment), and had to put into my mouth some gas tubing attached to a gas ring, which – magically – produced a flame when a match was applied. The whole contraption quite naturally had the foul smell (and taste) of coal gas and I can't believe that anyone present could have taken it seriously as a conjuring trick. I also had to demonstrate a 'magic' light bulb which lit up when you held it – very original.

My father used to take me up to London during the holidays to the Maskelyne and Devant magic shows or to an ice show; on one occasion (I think it was at Bertram Mills' Circus at Earls Court) we witnessed a horrendous accident. A stunt motorcyclist rode round the inside of a large wire cage (rather like the 'wall of death' at a fairground), and then the cage was raised up to quite some height above the ring and a large trap door was opened; all this time the motorcyclist was still going round and round, of course. Then disaster struck: his shirt became entangled in the rear wheel of the bike, he inevitably slowed down and, before the trap door could be shut, he plummeted to his death in the sawdust ring beneath in full view of the enormous crowd. I have never been to a circus since.

During the summer holiday of 1950, I went with the Greens to my first air display, at Lee-on-Solent; it was a typical British summer's day, and as a respite from the pouring rain it was suggested that we went for a pleasure flight. I had never flown before, but there was no time to think about it or to decide whether to be scared or not, because within a matter of minutes we were being bundled into a Dragon Rapide (or more accurately a naval Dominie, almost certainly NF854) and were airborne.

This flight kindled more interest, and in 1951 I paid the occasional visit to Fair Oaks, where I was able to photograph the 18 RFTS Ansons and Chipmunks as well as some of the aircraft belonging to Universal Flying Services. Unfortunately there must have been something wrong with the viewfinder of my camera as all the photos came out with the right-hand side of the subject missing.

Also in 1951 David Timmis and I had a day out at the Festival of Britain Exhibition (famous for its skylons, nylons, pylons etc.); in particular I remember that the DH.88 Comet G-ACSS had been restored to static condition for the event. Aeroplanes were becoming more important to me.

Even in these days of relative affluence in the UK, with millions taking to the air to search out the sun in foreign parts, there is still a feeling of awe and excitement about one's first flight, and this has always been particularly the case in a light aircraft where you are so close to the elements. All I can remember is that as a result of that Dominie flight and my visits to Fair Oaks I was well and truly 'bitten' by the aeroplane bug, although being only about thirteen I was obviously in no position to do anything more about furthering my interests in a practical way. However, that was to change before long.

CHAPTER 3
LANCING DAYS
(1951-1955)

For some reason my parents must have thought that I had an academic bent, because in 1950 I was persuaded by them to try for an entrance scholarship to Winchester College. To do this it was necessary to attend in person along with all the other candidates. It was a stiflingly hot summer and Winchester, lying in a natural hollow, seemed to be the hottest place on earth; we students, restrained behind desks in an old oak-panelled hall for the best part of two days, simmered gently. My mother and I stayed for two nights in a B & B establishment run by a Mrs Bruin; we were offered only the bare essentials.

After this ordeal was over I must confess that I was rather relieved to discover that I was rated almost last out of about sixty-five entrants: I had no desire to become a Wykehamist. I was next persuaded to sit the Common Entrance exam for Lancing College. This time there was no need for me actually to go there, but I can recall being cooped up on my own in a small room at Cottesmore for hours on end, staring at pieces of printed paper and occasionally committing something to plain white foolscap. To my lasting surprise, this time I was somewhat more successful and managed to come second equal with Colin Johnson, earning a reduction in the annual fees of £75 – not a small sum in those days, and hopefully worthwhile assistance for my parents, who had not found things easy financially. Prospect of a further spell at boarding school did not worry me unduly as I had already spent so much of my young life in Sussex that I considered the county almost as my second home.

So it was that in September of 1951 I found myself once more on a train, this time bound (eventually) for Shoreham station. I preferred using the train at the beginning and end of each term to having my father drive me down. There were two possible routes from Woking to Shoreham, and I usually took the quicker (though longer) one, which involved changing trains at Havant, and then travelling along the south coast via Chichester and Worthing to Shoreham; the trains were electric and fairly fast and comfortable. However on one occasion I decided by way of a change to sample the geographically shorter route; this involved changing trains twice, first at Guildford, then at Horsham, finally boarding a real anachronism, nicknamed the "Steyning Flier," which was hauled by a small black tank engine and ambled gently between the South

Downs to Shoreham and eventually Brighton. The two red coaches were claimed to be well over fifty years old, and in my experience they certainly lived up to that reputation, as the design was definitely Victorian; many of the seats suffered with horsehair hernias and the sliding compartment doors came off their runners at the slightest provocation, as I soon found out. Although I still find it difficult even today to comprehend all the reasons behind the severe cuts instigated by Doctor Beeching during the sixties, I have never had a real problem in seeing why he must have decided to axe this particular branch line; nevertheless, if only it remained today it would doubtless have become a money-spinner catering for the tourist trade.

In time I, along with other more senior pupils, was allowed to keep a bicycle at the school, and this of course was a great aid to independence for any teenager. Cycling was also one very enjoyable (though tiring) way of travelling from home to school and vice versa, and I tried it on several occasions. First my luggage would be sent on by train (it never got lost) and then I would launch myself into the ride, which was about 42 miles in length; the route passed through some beautiful Surrey and Sussex countryside and also right past Dunsfold aerodrome, by now the home of Hawker Aircraft.

It didn't take me long to learn a unchangeable piece of weather lore, which was that the direction in which you are travelling on a bicycle is of no signifcance as the wind is always against you! That bicycle cost me £17 brand-new in 1951 and proved so sturdy that I disposed of it only in 1986.

Those readers who have not attended a public school (I always maintain with a certain degree of cynicism that such an upbringing prepares you best for a career culminating either in politics or prison, and occasionally both) may wonder what Lancing College was like to live and work in. In the physical sense Lancing College sat atop one of the South Downs and comprised (as indeed it still does today with some modern additions) a large number of exceptionally solid-looking stone and flint buildings, linked together on different levels by cloistered passageways, staircases and quadrangles. The enormous Chapel, as large as many cathedrals, continually reminded us that there were meant to be other sides to life than just the physical, and it stood like a brooding prehistoric monument on the top of the hill, unfinished since the previous century, and with a west end sporting the largest expanse of corrugated iron in England (or so we were told, as if it was something worthy of the Guinness Book of Records).

Another reminder that we were at Lancing to develop our character in adversity was that, wherever we went throughout the school complex, we couldn't seem to get away from the draughts.

To a teenager, life at such a school in an environment with an air of permanent monasticism about it presented some strange paradoxes. For example, personal cleanliness, grooming and good manners were considered very important as, after all, we were being prepared to fit into society; yet we were encouraged to go on cross-country runs through a selection of muddy fields and deep water-filled ditches (dykes), so that even after a bath or shower all our colleagues still knew exactly what we had been doing that afternoon. We were also encouraged to develop the skills of leadership and show initiative, yet any slight bending or infringement of the school rules in the intended interest of efficiency or expediency could easily result in the use of the cane. However, despite today's pundits who tell us that corporal punishment can never be justified, I can't say that it ever did any of us any lasting harm; what I do know is that the skin-hardening properties of methylated spirits (when rubbed on externally, not taken internally) quickly became common knowledge. If nothing else we learned the value of self-discipline, a quality which will stand any individual in good stead all his life.

On the whole the food was remarkably good and there was certainly plenty of it. The school boasted its own bakery, so we enjoyed the luxury of fresh bread every day, and also cake at weekends; the delicious aromas pervaded all the nearby buildings. We also had our own personal 'tuckboxes' at school; these were wooden hampers kept full of extra foods and special treats brought or sent from home, so it is fair to say we never needed to go hungry! However we were kept in reasonable shape by the vigorous exercise that we underwent every day, which could take any one of a number of forms; in the main I opted for running, swimming, football, fives or squash (our Housemaster was the well-known squash player and coach Sam Jagger, who had written educational books on the sport).

I had made up my mind when a lot younger that I wanted to study science, and especially chemistry, and at Lancing my opportunity had now come. Fortunately we had teachers who knew how to get the best out of their pupils and could give them the attention they needed, and so it is not surprising that with that encouragement I have followed a career involving chemistry all my working life. At the end of my first year of studying the subject, my aspirations were vindicated when I was awarded 100% marks in the examination by our teacher, Mr Brand – never equalled or even approached since then, I hasten to add.

One day in the science laboratory I made a chance discovery that provided some amusement: I found that if I blew hard down the gas tubing, all the lit Bunsen burners on the bench went out after about fifteen seconds or so. There was a tall rack of shelves filled with reagent bottles along the middle of the bench which screened me from anyone working on the other side, so after blowing hard I would wander round casually to see whoever was working on the other side of the bench and ask them how their experiment was progressing. As they were about to pass comment the Bunsen would inexplicably extinguish itself, and of course I was just as surprised as they were.

The teaching staff were all very memorable characters, one of the most enigmatic being the school's Vice-Chaplain, Henry Thorold, a classical scholar with a dry wit and renowned for his careful choice of words, some of them pronounced incorrectly purely for the sake of effect; many were the times he amused us with his wit during his lessons (and sometimes his sermons too). Speaking of the latter, I can remember clearly the opening words from one such sermon: "Soup, seven-and-six." What the rest of the sermon was about I haven't the faintest idea, but this phrase has for some reason stuck firmly in my mind, I suppose because in the early fifties such a sum represented a ridiculously high figure to be asked to pay for a basic commodity such as a plate of soup. Perhaps that was just the point: for all I know, he may have gone on to show, for example, that some things in life are not worth the sacrifice you are being asked to make – very profound maybe, but probably quite wrong.

On one summer afternoon he invited a small group of students to his rooms to share a special 'strawberries and cream' tea; after all his young guests had wolfed down their share, one of them noticed that his host had not as yet touched his strawberries but was just sitting there looking at them. When the lad tried to encourage him by saying: "Go on, sir, why haven't you eaten yours yet?", he turned his head slowly, fixed the questioner with a beady eye, and in carefully measured tones made the solemn pronouncement: "The anticipation of the *pleesure* [sic] is almost as great as the *pleesure* itself."

Although intended just to raise a smile there was, on reflection, a deeper significance to this statement which has stayed with me through the years, for how true this principle has turned out to be in life for almost all of us; indeed sometimes the anticipation of a pleasure proves to be even better than the thing or event when it finally *does* arrive, as anyone who has changed a car or house, or ordered a slap-up meal at a strongly-recommended restaurant, can testify.

Mr Thorold's 'boss,' the Chaplain, Wilf Derry, conformed more to what we considered the norm of behaviour. The tedium which was bound to set in from time to time during his sermons was relieved only by one thing, our noticing his habit of taking off his glasses at fairly regular intervals and then replacing them again a moment later. It was only to be expected therefore that some of us who, I must confess, were not really too concerned at the time about our spiritual development, and were only waiting for the final prayer to finish so that we could get out, capitalised on this minor diversion and began to keep records of the number of times he followed this routine during each sermon. Would he break the record this week? Would he drop his glasses and tread on them whilst looking for them so he would not be able to continue his sermon? These and other questions kept us fully occupied. I believe that we may have even taken bets. What Philistines we must have been!

But since those days I have often pondered about the effects that having to attend Chapel once every day and twice on Sundays had on us. I would reason that if this way of worship, which was very high church, was indeed the right one (I have always felt that surely there must be only one correct religion), then the truth should have encouraged more, and not less, interest in the pupils as time went by.

Sex and morality were issues that seldom surfaced openly at boarding schools in the fifties. Today I suppose that, in a boarding school for adolescent boys only, the staff would have to expect all sorts of problems of a moral nature, including homosexuality, to crop up fairly regularly, yet in the fifties there was a general atmosphere of innocence if not downright naivety. Although such nefarious activities almost certainly did occur from time to time, they were kept very quiet indeed, *so* quiet that on one occasion my parents received a letter from the headmaster accusing me of being the ring-leader of a group; I had been well and truly framed! It was fortunate that I was able to explain my innocence (which was the truth) to his satisfaction and that, happily, was the end of the matter.

However, under the rather constrained circumstances it was not easy to develop in the social graces. One of the greatest mysteries concerned the ballroom-dancing classes. Practising dance steps with another boy as a partner, especially if you had to dance backwards, was not looked upon with favour by those who were told to do it (and possibly didn't help any immoral leanings which might be just below the surface). I recall an incident in one episode of the TV comedy "Steptoe and Son" where Harold's first dance, to which he had been looking forward so much, was completely ruined for him because he had not realised that his father had been teaching him the lady's steps.

In an attempt to preserve some sort of 'normality' we were offered a School Dance, and this was held every term with a special event for the end of each summer term. The School Dance took place during an evening when a selection of local girls, chosen for their impeccable family and moral backgrounds, were invited to the school to provide us with real live dancing partners. However, after the first time we experienced such a Dance the thrill waned as we came to understand the principles involved in this highly pre-organised confrontation of the sexes.

The girls were provided with chairs along one side of the school hall, where they sat looking suitably demure but shyly giggling amongst themselves; the boys, who were not provided with such luxuries as chairs, lounged against the opposite wall whispering to each other and eyeing up the girls, as was only to be expected. When the Victor Silvester record started we had to make it across the hall to secure the partner we had had our eye on before anyone else could beat us to it. As we were forbidden to carry on conversation with our chosen partner, dancing progressed without there being any opportunity to exchange even the simplest of pleasantries. Once the music stopped all of us were expected to return to our appointed places immediately and stay there until the procedure was repeated with the next record, the only difference then being in the tempo of the music.

Needless to say, this official approach to social mixing was not appreciated by us (nor indeed was it meant to be, probably), but for certain there was never any opportunity for trouble! It appears that this practice continued for some years, as George Miles mentioned to me in a letter a few years ago that his daughter was a guest at these dances in about 1960.

From then on I maintained a healthy disrespect for the pastime of dancing (and have in fact done so all my life, although ironically I still play keyboard music for dancing to this day). Of course this was an impractical stance to adopt, as such an attitude towards dancing was hardly to be an aid to courting in later years. In those days dances were the most common way of meeting the girl of your dreams!

In the enlightened nineties there are now girl boarders at Lancing along with the boys, although at least decency dictates separate accommodation, I am happy to say. There have been great changes in attitudes to morality during the past forty years, but how many of them have really been for the better?

Being an only child I had become quite used to amusing myself for a lot of the time. There seemed to be lots of hours to spare in those days (although in fairness we worked hard during the time prescribed for it) and most of the weekend from Saturday lunchtime onwards was ours apart from the obligatory Chapel services on Sundays. I got into the habit of bringing my Hornby Dublo model railway from home, and combined it with track belonging to other boys to make a really big layout in the loft over the armoury. I also became involved with making scale models of model aircraft out of balsa wood (carved from scratch out of blocks, not made from kits), and finished up with quite a large collection which was kept at home. Many of these model aircraft are now displayed in the Museum of Berkshire Aviation as even at the age of fifteen I had a fondness for Miles designs. I also built and flew diesel-powered control-line models on the playing fields, clocking up over 80 mph with one of them.

My diary at the time records some details of how I used to spend my carefully eked-out pocket money for the term. We were free to supplement our diet (either at the school tuck shop or in local towns) and I also used to spend time and money in the local model shop. In 1953-54 typical prices were as follows:

Packet of biscuits	10d
1 lb pot of jam	1/4d
Packet of clear gums	3d
Packet of fruit pastilles	3d
Clear dope	1/6d
Small paint brush	9d
Balsa cement	6d
Plastic wood	1/-
Packet of sandpaper	1/-
Sheet of 1/8 in balsa wood	1/1d
Biro refill	1/4d
Cinema ticket	2/3d
Hair cut	1/6d

On "Saints' Days" we were given most of the day off from midmorning onwards (I wasn't aware that the Church of England recognised these, but we still considered the practice one of the more enlightened features of our religious education); we were given permission to take the bus (or our bike) to the nearby towns of Shoreham, Lancing or Worthing. I took full advantage of this provision and must have seen almost every new film released during the early fifties at one or other of the Worthing cinemas. I can remember the "Dome" on the seafront, but I think there was a "Classic" too. I have also enjoyed many of these films more recently on television, especially ones with an aviation theme such as "The Sound Barrier" and "No Highway."

It was obligatory at Lancing to join the Cadet Force, and everyone had to spend the first year in the Army section. Apart from the inevitable drill practices, instruction on how to clean uniform buttons and belts with Duraglit and pulling a piece of 'four-by-two' through the barrel of a ·303 rifle, we were occasionally given duties on the outdoor shooting range, which more often than not meant being sent to the receiving end of the range with instructions to hold up a pointer on a long stick to indicate which part of the target had been hit (if anyone managed to be that accurate.). Another frequent detail was to march to the top of nearby Boiler Hill (a local trig point) and learn how to identify local geographical features from a large map.

I have come across an essay I wrote in 1954, which described this activity; it also gave me an opportunity to publicise my interest in aviation. It was entitled "Maps" and the teacher's comment was: "Interesting and informative," which of course can cover almost anything.

MAPS

"'The best laid schemes of mice and men gang oft a-gley.'

This quotation could aptly be applied to the planning of a journey, for even after seemingly studiously consulting a map before setting out, motorists still get completely lost, and navigators have to admit to their respective pilots that their 'position is uncertain.'

There is a case, however, for both motorist and navigator. As for the latter, he cannot tell from inside an aircraft – without becoming involved in a great many complications – when the wind changes either its direction or its force without warning; so it is quite possible to drift miles off track. But the navigator, by observing the country over which he is flying, should be able to pick up his position on the map.

The motorist, on the other hand, is in a different position. Unless he is on top of some isolated hill, he obviously cannot easily pinpoint his position at once. Often the signposts manage somehow to confuse him more and more; and then he despairs and falls to the lowest depths – he asks someone to direct him. This someone is almost always either blind, a stranger to the district, or a foreigner.

The only thing to do is to carry on to the next crossroads, and then, on looking very carefully at the signposts and the names of places on them, with the distances in miles following, he should by referring to the map be able to find out exactly where he is. This method works at night and in fogs also.

There are some people who do not seem to be able to read maps at all. Any attempts to pick out details always seem to be fruitless. Schools provide for this by incorporating a Map-Reading Section in the CCF [Combined Cadet Force]. Diligent instructors continually try to drill into cadets' heads such things as conventional signs, orientation, grid lines and magnetic north.

One special treat on an extraordinarily fine day used to be for the squad to be marched up to the top of Boiler Hill, where each member would be equipped with an old and ragged map provided by the instructor. The squad, on the word of command "Fall Out," would rapidly fade away into neighbouring shrubbery, until called back into sight by the irate instructor.

The order would then be given for each person to 'orient' his map on Shoreham Church and Cowtop [a prominent hill about two miles north]. When these two landmarks were aligned correctly, it would be time to be marched back down to the College.

As the maps were being handed in, the wind would come in opportune gusts, and various sheets of paper would be seen either caught in the barbed wire fence, or floating gracefully over the adjoining field. A grand interlude would follow, when eventually, all maps collected, the poor boys would arrive back at the College late for tea.

The question of surveying land has always been something of a problem, and one answer has been found. Recently three helicopters with appropriate apparatus and crew surveyed an area in Alaska in fifteen days. When this area was last surveyed, from land, it took three years. A small company at Shoreham Airport, Meridian Airmaps Ltd, is doing the same kind of work [with the Aerovan G-AJKP], and there are many other similar companies.

Certainly, surveying by air should be the answer to the cry for up-to-date maps."

Team sports, as at Cottesmore, did not occupy more of my time than was absolutely necessary. However, we had a good swimming pool, and I was also taught squash and fives. Our housemaster, Sam Jagger, was an expert at the former, and for my size and weight I like to think I became reasonably proficient in time. Cross-country running was frequently on the agenda; I was not too keen on this, having done what I thought was my share at Cottesmore, but sometimes I had to give in. One feature of cross-country running (mentioned earlier) which I despised was having to go through the dykes, the deep and wide ditches that were common at field edges; the problem was you didn't know quite how deep they were, nor had you any idea what (either animate or inanimate in nature) might be lurking beneath the water. I always preferred planned walks around the local downs: on a Sunday we used to cover several miles, stopping to eat our packed lunch on the way (packed lunches could be ordered for Sundays in advance from the school kitchens). We were also permitted to play golf on the local courses at Hove or Worthing, which was another beneficial form of exercise.

Being allowed to keep a bicycle at school was to prove very advantageous to someone with my interests; of course Shoreham aerodrome itself was classified as out of bounds, but needless to say this did not stop anyone riding round the perimeter track on their way to and from a legitimate destination such as Shoreham town centre!

But in 1952 when I began my new hobby of aircraft spotting I was not old enough to be allowed to keep my bicycle at school and still enjoyed walking anyway. One of my school friends was Tim Foster, who emigrated to Canada in 1956, and only returned to the UK in the mid-eighties – it was a great pleasure to meet up with him again recently. Tim was a member of a relatively new organisation called Air-Britain founded as recently as 1948, and it was him that I must thank for introducing me to the hobby of 'spotting' that I have followed, as circumstances have permitted, throughout all the years since. Although I had shown quite a lot of interest previously, and still had the photographs I had taken at Fair Oaks the previous year, I had never considered as particularly significant the lettering or serial numbers on individual aircraft, any more than many people today bother to remember the details of car number-plates, even their own!

On Sunday 22nd June 1952 Tim and I went on our first 'spotting' trip to Shoreham, and from that day to this I have kept a diary, the contents of which (in as far as they relate to activities connected with aviation) have provided the basis for many of the Appendices to this book.

CHAPTER 4
A LIFETIME'S HOBBY BEGINS
(MID-1952–MID-1955)

Situated on the South Coast between Shoreham & Worthing, and owned jointly by the local municipal authorities for over sixty years, Shoreham must be one of the best-known aerodromes in the UK. Now, of course, it boasts a tarmac runway, but back in the 1950s there was no such facility; some may prefer it the way it was, but at least the aerodrome does not now get completely waterlogged and unserviceable as it used to, in late 1954 for example. I remember that after ten days or so of gales and heavy rain in late November and early December the airfield was still officially closed when one afternoon the Proctor G-AIWA landed, throwing up clouds of spray as it did so; needless to say, the pilot received a severe reprimand from Air Traffic Control for disobeying signals.

A 1955 publication gave the essential details of the aerodrome simply as follows:

"5 miles E. by N. of Worthing. Elevation, 10 ft. Grass Area, N-S 800 yds; NE-SW 1,100 yds; E-W 930 yds; SE-NW 830 yds."

When flying to Shoreham, the most dramatic approach is almost certainly from the north, when you come through the Shoreham Gap, leaving Lancing College with its dominating Chapel to your right. In the fifties another landmark was the cement works near Steyning in the valley just north of the aerodrome, whose smoking chimneys could be seen from many miles away and gave you an early warning of the wind direction. Normally this is from approximately the south-west, so you drop over the old toll-bridge on the river Adur and flare out onto the field. It is indeed a beautiful setting and as popular a venue for private flyers now as it was in the 1950s.

What a visitor will likely notice more than anything if returning after an absence of some years is, firstly, the enormous number of light and business aircraft permanently parked in the open, and secondly, the predominance of American aircraft almost to the exclusion of anything of British origin; but of course this scenario is not peculiar to Shoreham.

In the early fifties it was very different: there were not more than about a dozen resident aircraft at Shoreham, and all of them, and indeed almost all of the visiting aircraft, were British-built. While I make no claims to be a patriot (to me it seems that national pride has done little to further the cause of world peace in this century, or any other – but I'm sure I'm treading on dangerous ground here!), I think that a lot of the flying fraternity would agree with me when I say that I deeply regret the effective demise of a commercial and innovative British light aircraft industry when Beagle Aircraft finally folded in the late sixties.

In the fifties virtually every type of light aircraft flying in any numbers was built by one of four Companies: Auster, de Havilland, Miles or Percival. To my mind, all the aircraft built in the thirties, forties and fifties have a shape and style that epitomises what an aeroplane *should* look like; today they would be called 'classics,' I suppose, some of them even 'vintage,' and they command a great deal of well-deserved attention wherever they turn up.

Has there really been such an improvement in performance, comfort, reliability and economy since those days, even with the continuing tidal wave of modern American imports? In 1992 *"Flyer"* magazine compared the Percival Vega Gull (built in the mid-thirties) with the Piper Cherokee Arrow then current. Although it has a greater take-off weight, the Vega Gull carries a third more useful load, has a quicker rate of climb, and has take-off and landing runs of about half that of its modern counterpart! *"Flyer"* concluded that, notwithstanding its non-retractable undercarriage, its heavier and less economical engine, and the fact that its design was not far off sixty years old, "the Vega Gull runs rings around the Arrow." So what really is progress?

In the early fifties other rarer machines were seen at Shoreham including the prewar Dart Kitten G-AEXT, the Spartan Arrow G-ABWP, the Chilton G-AFSV and the BA Swallow G-AFHS; these caused me great excitement when I saw them actually flying, but American-built machines such as Piper Cubs and the Aeronca Champion N79854 (later G-AOEH), although rare indeed in those days, did not seem to generate quite the same enthusiasm in me.

Friday afternoons were at first earmarked for the Army section of the Cadet Force (as mentioned earlier), but after my first year it was possible to join the Air Force section instead, and this made life a lot more interesting, as we were taught things I considered useful, like meteorology, principles of flight and aircraft recognition. I was made Flight Sergeant in charge of the Cadets during my last year at school, although I suspect that this may have been a case of "Hobson's Choice" for the CO, Bill Dovell.

In about March 1953 I made my first of several visits to RNAS Ford, in an entirely private capacity. Then on June the 13th, on an official visit by the school's Air Cadets, we had a flight in Anson

MH117. Just over a month later on the 25th July, I attended their annual display; for me, the highlights of these displays throughout the fifties inevitably included one of Lt. Cdr. Sproule's latest Heath Robinson-like creations dangling beneath a Dragonfly helicopter and carrying a very brave soul in fancy dress. I have included some details of these visits in Appendix 5.

On several afternoons during the second half of May I saw large formations of Lincoln bombers flying along the south coast over Shoreham at not more than about 1,000 feet in an easterly direction; these flights were in rehearsal for the Coronation Flypast over London on the 2nd June. As Lincolns had an all-black finish and carried huge white-painted serial numbers, it was possible to identify most of them, and details are given in Appendix 4.

At the end of the summer term, we were all sent off to Camp at RAF Cranwell. My diary records the list of things which we were told to pack: kitbag, groundsheet, emergency ration card, Service Record book, extra pair of shoes, extra pair of trousers, coat, towel, soap, toothbrush, toilet paper, change of underclothing, pair of gym shoes, swimming trunks, running vest, running shorts, knife, fork, spoon and drinking mug. This medley was all packed up and sent by rail, so my diary tells me, addressed to: Cadet Campbell, Lancing College Contingent, CCF Summer Camp, c/o RAF Station, Cranwell, Lincolnshire.

We ourselves also went to Cranwell by train, directly from school, and arrived late on the 26th July. I can remember that, as could only be expected, we were kept pretty busy, but that the food and accommodation were not at all bad, considering. In accordance with standard Services procedure we had been ordered to salute any officer we should pass, and after a confusing incident the first afternoon shortly after leaving the NAAFI mess I had to remember that in future I should be sure to hold my cutlery and mug in my *left* hand!

On our second full day at Cranwell, the 28th July, a very important event took place at the College, although at the time I was not able to appreciate its full significance, except that I had an idea that it must be the annual Passing Out parade. Now, after some research all of forty-five years later, I know that it was indeed the annual Passing Out Parade, but made even more of a special occasion because, being Coronation Year, the Duke of Edinburgh had graciously accepted an invitation to attend.

So it was that the 28th July turned out to be one of the most serendipitous days of my young life. Despite changeable weather a large number aircraft descended on Cranwell South airfield, and to my surprise and delight we were allowed to wander around them all, quite unmolested, during lunchtime and the early afternoon.

Although most of the aircraft were service types, I remember discovering tucked away amongst the larger aircraft the Autocrat G-AJIE and the Miles Nighthawk G-AGWT (flown in by its owner, Wing Commander Grece). However, it is a pity that, out of all the records that I have kept since I first started 'spotting' in 1952, this event proves to be the only one where I have only very incomplete details of the aircraft present, as the grubby bit of paper that I recorded them all on must have been mislaid many years ago.

It has always been in my mind to try and obtain more information about this event. Recent correspondence with Jean Buckberry, the librarian and archivist at Cranwell, has revealed that there are no official records available detailing the aircraft attending on that day; in fact the only record that exists is an article which appeared later that year in the official College magazine, together with a number of photographic negatives. I was granted permission to quote from this article in my book *"Tail Ends of the Fifties,"* and also to use any of the negatives I wished; and so I eagerly awaited the set of some seventy negatives to arrive so that I could resolve some of the identities of the attending aircraft. But in reality it was of course the Duke who was the centre of attention on that day, not the aircraft, and the pictures taken reflect that; nevertheless I was able to directly confirm the identities of some of them.

Then, by checking and cross-checking my other records, I have done my best to produce as near a complete list as possible. At least the *numbers* of each type present are correct, although their *identities* are for the most part deduced rather than known for certain. The details are in Appendix 6.

During our stay we were also given flights in the College's Chipmunks (I flew in WK556 & WK567). Aerobatics were an entirely new experience for me; I remember that loops were actually quite enjoyable once you got used to them, but barrel rolls, which seemed to be one pilot's *pièce de resistance*, had me feeling queasy for the rest of the day.

On the last of our three days we were taken by coach for a quick visit to Skegness. At the time I knew that there was an aerodrome at Boston, so was very disappointed to see nothing as we went past. It was just as well that I didn't know about the existence of Ingoldmells aerodrome at Skegness, or I would have felt let down twice as much!

Later in the summer of 1953 I took my first holiday on my own. At the end of August I stayed at Eltham in SE London, in the family home of our erstwhile evacuee Joyce Honner. Eltham is to this day not widely known as a popular holiday venue, but for me it was ideal because I was easily able to get to Croydon and Biggin Hill by public transport.

A week or two later I was on my way to the Isle of Wight: my parents had friends in Seaview who provided Bed & Breakfast accommodation, and whilst there I was lent a bicycle so that, amongst other things, I could tour the three local aerodromes, Ryde, Sandown and Bembridge. Ryde was pretty well disused after the war but the green Autocrat G-AGYM was present there when I visited, possibly for pleasure-flying. Sandown produced a few interesting aircraft, particularly those of Bees Flight, while at Bembridge a Bristol Freighter (G-AIFV) was engaged in loading cars, the first time I had seen this exercise; and when I got back to Ryde Pier the Saunders Roe Princess G-ALUN obligingly flew over sufficiently low for me to photograph it.

On November 17th 1953 it must have been a "Saints' Day" holiday (see earlier), as I see from my diary that I took a train up to Gatwick because I had heard of some Seafires parked up there. I can recall vividly, even now, that when I arrived at the airfield the fog was almost impenetrable, with certainly less than fifty yards visibility. This actually made it easier to tour the aerodrome as it was highly unlikely that anyone would be telling me to clear off. The Seafires were indeed there, ten of them, along with two Sea Hornets (see Appendix 7). I have never found out where they came from or where they went – to the scrap heap, perhaps?

During the early years of the fifties most of the visiting aircraft at Shoreham were fairly small, but what they lacked in size they made up for in quantity. Highlights included Summer Camps with swarms of military Austers and Chipmunks, the development flying of the Sparrowjet G-ADNL, and a weekend visit in early 1954 by the extraordinary Hurel Dubois HD-31 (see later). Indeed it was that year that provided the first signs that larger aircraft were to use the airfield regularly. Dragon Rapides, Doves and a Prince were already fairly common visitors, then came the occasional DC-3 (one of which is featured on the front cover), and after that Provosts, Balliols, a Firefly and a Varsity.

I am fortunate enough to possess quite a few of the Movements Books from September 1954 onwards, together with information from other enthusiasts such as Fred Lynn, Keith Donald, Peter Amos and Philip Ansell; from this I have been able to build up a picture of Shoreham activities between 1945 and 1970, which I have published as a separate venture.

One of the most interesting visitors of the decade must have been the Herald G-AODE on the 11th June 1957. A couple of years later, on the 30th May 1959, even a Blackburn Beverley – together with many other exotic types – graced Shoreham's grass in connection with a RAFA Air Display.

The Sparrowjet was a Turboméca Palas-powered conversion of the prewar Sparrowhawk G-ADNL and retained the same registration despite an almost total rebuild. It first flew in this configuration on the 14th December 1953 piloted by George Miles, and was intended to be raced by Fred Dunkerley, owner of Gemini G-AKKB (now one of the only two airworthy Geminis in the UK and operated by Jim Buckingham from Bristol). After narrowly avoiding a nasty accident on the 7th June 1954, the Sparrowjet flew spasmodically throughout the summer (I believe that this was due to problems with the engines), took part in the Goodyear Trophy Race on the 28th August, and was flown by Airspeed's chief test pilot on the 25th October. Thereafter it had a rather chequered career, not being as successful on the racing scene as had been hoped. One of the drawbacks was the amount of time that it took to get up to full speed, as the thrust from the small jets was not by any means excessive (330 lb each), and so handicapping effectively ruled out a good final place.

Eventually it did win the King's Cup race at Coventry in 1957 at a speed of 228 mph, the first jet aircraft ever to achieve this. Sad to say, I missed that particular race as I was in hospital in London having my tonsils out (what abominable timing!); a great shame as the race was unique in postwar years in that Miles aircraft took five of the first six places; the interloper in second place was the Percival Mew Gull, which we can forgive, but the next four places were taken by a Falcon Six, a Monarch, a Hawk Trainer and a Gemini.

In 1955 I made a scale model of the Sparrowjet and entered it in a local handicrafts competition held in the autumn, which was officially opened by comedian Fred Emney, who lived nearby. A highlight of the exhibition was a public demonstration of two-way radio communication with an Anson of the RAF which was flying overhead. I am pleased to say that my model was awarded first prize in the aeromodelling section, and is one of the models displayed in the Museum of Berkshire Aviation that I mentioned earlier.

The Sparrowjet was eventually retired, and acquired by the Nash Aeronautical collection at Heathrow, where it was stored in the BEA Engineering base. After being moved to Upavon it was destroyed by a hangar fire in 1964, and this, one would have thought, was the end of the story. So in 1992 I was extremely surprised to see the registration G-ADNL restored as a Miles Sparrowhawk to a certain Kathleen Dunkerley (who I believe is Fred's daughter). I now understand that, using all the original metal parts which were not required in 1953 and then stored, Ben Cox is well on the way to producing a Sparrowhawk once again to take to the air.

Another of 1954's visitors, the Hurel Dubois HD-31, was unusual, to say the least; it had an enormous wingspan for its weight, and had been designed to investigate the phenomenon of decreased drag at low cruising speeds when using a very high aspect-ratio wing. It arrived at Shoreham on the 25th March and stayed over until the 28th of March for a press and sales demonstration; F.G. Miles Ltd later converted one of their Aerovans (G-AJOF) to a similar configuration, when it was re-registered G-AHDM. An official *"Aeroplane"* photograph of the HD-31 taken at the time has a special significance for me; a reproduction of it appears elsewhere in this book, and I can assure you that I personally appear in the picture! Of the two small figures leaning on bicycles, I am the one on the left with my back to the camera, talking to my friend David Martin. I have listed details of the aircraft present that weekend in Appendix 8.

Two other Miles-inspired developments were exhibited in the main concourse of the terminal building. One was a lightweight glider wing made of phenolic and asbestos fibre materials stabilized with a paper honeycomb in the centre; this had been intended for a high-performance glider which was to be entered in the 1954 World Gliding Championships and flown by Hugh Kendall, but in the event it was never fitted. The other was a stainless steel model of the M.52 supersonic research aircraft that had been axed by the government just after the war. At the time the public were told that it was such an advanced venture that it would not be fair to ask any pilot to accept the risk. Another reason given was that documents captured in Germany at the end of the war indicated that all German research into supersonic flight favoured a swept-wing configuration whereas the M.52 had razor-thin *unswept* wings. Don Brown (whom I had the privilege of meeting once with my schoolfriend Peter Keeling when we visited him at Powerjets at Farnborough) says in his book *"Miles Aircraft Since 1925"*:

" . . . in February 1946, over two years of concentrated and dedicated work . . . was thrown away, together with over £100,000 of taxpayers' money: and by this cancellation, Great Britain threw away the honour of being the first nation to achieve supersonic flight."

Similar scenarios been repeated over and over again in this country, especially in aviation. The real reasons for the cancellation of the project have been under debate for many years and have only recently become more clear, thanks to a lot of hard work by Dennis Bancroft.

But now back to the fifties. Much of our weekday spotting took place from the balcony of the chapel, where we could get quite a good view of the aerodrome, although we needed more than ordinary binoculars to make any positive identifications. Fortunately my father had lent me his ex-WW I telescope with a 30 x magnification, but this was very heavy and needed to be supported on the parapet of the balcony to keep it steady.

However Sundays were special as we were free for most of the day. Whenever a Sunday was fine enough for flying (there seemed to be a lot more of them in those days) and the ritual of morning chapel was over, I would meet up with a fellow enthusiast (generally Tim Foster, David Timmis, Nick Rose or John Hill) and complete our preparations for a day out. We took a packed lunch, our binoculars (mine came from Paddington Station Lost Property Office for the princely sum of £5) and in the cooler weather a small Primus stove for making hot drinks. Then we strolled down the College drive and across the fields to a long natural bank near the Sussex Pad Hotel which faced south over the A27 and overlooked the whole of the aerodrome. Sadly this superb vantage point is no longer in existence as it was bulldozed away some years ago when the road was widened into a dual carriageway.

We normally arrived at about 11.30 and were able to stay until just before 5.30 pm, so we managed to witness most of the aerial activities of the day. Our snacks and drinks were very welcome during our vigil, and Sunday afternoons in the summer months were enlivened by the regular arrival at about three o'clock of the Alpine Ices van, whose driver grew used to our appearing out of the shrubbery and flagging him down; his orange ice-cream brickettes, sandwiched between two wafers, were a taste experience never to be forgotten!

Generally, aircraft landed from our left down the valley onto the NE-SW prepared strip, but sometimes the direction of the wind necessitated otherwise, and when it blew from a south-easterly direction it was always a great thrill when one of the Southern Aero Club's Hawk Trainers (G-AITS or G-AIZK) throttled back and slipped in right over our heads at less than fifty feet above us. I can also vividly remember the Messenger 4A G-ALBE doing likewise, with much spluttering and popping of the exhausts as it passed overhead with the engine throttled right back.

On this bank we had a virtually uninterrupted view all around, and were able to hear approaching aircraft from quite a long way off, before they could be seen with the naked eye. Even today I am delighted to confirm that I can still identify the distinctive note of a Gipsy Major engine about three miles distant, a very friendly and relaxing sound in a blue summer sky. How grateful we can be that there are still so many dedicated owners and engineers around who are determined to keep aircraft of this period flying.

We also came to recognise the probable aerodrome of departure of a visiting aircraft as it came into view from a particular point of the compass. If it came down the valley from the north-north-east, it would likely be from Croydon, Denham, Panshanger, Gatwick or Redhill: from the east, Rochester or Southend: from the north straight over the school, Fair Oaks or White Waltham: from over the hills to the north-west, Thruxton or Middle Wallop: and along the coast from the west, Portsmouth, Christchurch or Eastleigh. The activities on the aerodrome were punctuated at fairly regular intervals (except during the winter months) by the arrival and departure of Dragon Rapides – and later, Doves – on scheduled flights operated by East Anglian Flying Services (see Appendix 1).

During the mid-fifties a number of Flying Clubs used Shoreham fairly regularly as a cross-country destination, the most common aircraft seen being either Auster variants, Tiger Moths or Hawk Trainers, with the occasional Hornet Moth. Amongst these Clubs were Airways Aero Associations, Christchurch Aero Club, Croydon Flying Club, Experimental Flying Group, Ford RNVR Flying Group, Hampshire Aeroplane Club, Hookwood Flying Group, London Aero Club, Nightscale Flying Services, Penguin Flying Club, Royal Artillery Aero Club, Royal Naval Flying Club, Short Bros & Harland Flying Club, Southern Flying Schools, Surrey Aviation, Universal Flying Services and Wiltshire School of Flying. Most, if not all, of those names are with us no longer, but their mention will doubtless stir up some memories for any reader who was involved with aviation at that time.

Other regular movements involved the Dragon Rapides of Don Everall Aviation and Marshall's Flying Services, together with the Gemini of Flightways, usually flown by Hugh Kennedy; these were used to ferry jockeys, trainers etc. to and from the regular race meetings at Brighton Racecourse.

We soon got to recognise the various Club colour schemes as many painted their aircraft in distinctive colours in those days. A list of the Club-owned aircraft commonly seen at Shoreham, together with their colour schemes (as I remember them), is included in Appendix 2.

Apart from the activities on the aerodrome itself, many aircraft flew over the area, some of them quite unusual. The majority of Service aircraft were from the Royal Naval Air Station at Ford, near Bognor Regis; these included Attackers, Avengers, Fireflies, Gannets, Sea Balliols, Sea Furies, Sea Hawks, Sea Princes, Dragonfly helicopters, Vampire Trainers and Wyverns. Others, such as Marathons, Meteors and Varsities, came from Tangmere or Thorney Island, and even Farnborough provided the occasional *rara avis*, such as the all-red Lincoln WD125, the Derwent-Lincoln SX971, the Varsity prototype VX828, the Eland-Varsity VX835 and the Meteor 4 RA490 (deflected-jet testbed).

Other regular sightings included the Air Service Training fleet of DC-3s, Oxfords, Chipmunks and Austers, which often used Shoreham as a turning point but never landed there until the Auster 5 G-AKXP did so on the 17th June 1957.

On June 30th 1954 there was a partial eclipse of the sun at about 3 pm. I can recall the feeling of twilight, and all the birds started to make their evening roosting noises. All flying stopped for over an hour during the afternoon.

Advertising by banner-towing was quite common, and I well remember seeing the message "Right Monkey" being borne over our heads in huge red letters behind the Auster 5 G-AJAK, and wondering what it could be advertising as it made no sense to me! It was only later that I discovered that the comedian Al Read, whose catchphrase this was, was doing his summer show in Brighton. Another message towed by G-AJAK was "Suntan with Nylon." Some years later, just before banner-towing was prohibited, I remember seeing the green and white Lamtex Rugs' Prentice G-AOKH towing from Shoreham.

An unusual flight that I enjoyed in 1954 was as the result of a competition in the *"Evening Standard"* newspaper, which during

1953–55 operated a bright red Sikorsky S.51 helicopter G-ANAL (a registration that was changed to G-ANZL in March 1955, presumably because it was considered that some people might find it offensive). I entered the competition without any thought that I might actually be adjudged a winner, writing an essay on the theme provided, appropriately entitled "Why I Would Like to Fly in the *'Evening Standard'* Helicopter"; so I was very surprised indeed to be picked as one of the twenty-five lucky winners. On Sunday the 18th July time away from school was granted for me to make the flight from Croydon, and although it lasted for only eight minutes I had now flown in a helicopter, a rare privilege in those days for a schoolboy. As my film-star 'heart-throb' in those days was Jean Simmons, I was pleasantly surprised to find shortly before the flight that one of my fellow passengers bore that name, but alas! a meeting with the great star was not to be.

It must have been during this year that I first heard parts of the "Goon Show." I know that at the time I didn't have my own study (or 'pit'), and one evening I was strolling through the quadrangles on my way, eventually, to the communal toilets (euphemistically referred to as 'the groves') when I heard raised voices on the radio inside the study of a prefect. This turned out to be my introduction to the world of Eccles, Bluebottle, Neddie Seagoon, Moriarty, Gritpype-Thynne, Major Bloodnok etc. etc. The humour was more than appealing, it became essential to adjust one's mind and approach to life to accommodate it. I did manage to attend two live recordings of the show later on.

During the summer holidays I made a special journey back to Shoreham to attend the Goodyear Trophy Air Race Day on the 28th August; I stayed with my schoolfriend Peter Keeling in Worthing overnight. The weather was good, and the day suitably exhilarating; I took a number of photographs of the aircraft present, a few of which can be seen elsewhere in this book.

During the time I was a member of the RAF section of the school's Cadet Force I was given several opportunities to fly; once or twice a year an Anson from RAF Kenley would come to Shoreham to give Air Experience flights to some of us. Kenley's Ansons could always be recognised by their yellow spinners, and two examples in which I flew were PH528 and PH606.

Normally there was a telephone call earlier in the day to warn us that an aircraft would be coming, but one Friday afternoon we were heavily engaged in assembling the school's primary glider (of which more in the next chapter) when I couldn't help noticing a yellow-spinnered Anson flying low down the valley, obviously intent on landing at Shoreham. Fortunately I had sufficient credentials as a spotter to be able to convince our instructor, Bill Dovell our science teacher, that it had come for *us*, and we hastily left everything just as it was and ran (or 'sweated' might be a more appropriate verb) in our uniforms to the aerodrome a mile or more away; it was just as well for me that on this occasion I happened to be right, or my life would have been made a misery!

Other events entirely unconnected with aviation also came and went at school. We used to have regular film shows, and visiting musicians and actors came to entertain. I particularly remember the singer and raconteur Ian Wallace, who went down very well with us; seeing him on the television now, nearly fifty years later, he doesn't seem to have changed a bit! The composer Benjamin Britten and singer Peter Peers, both old boys of the school, also performed. We were very privileged to have a visit by John Betjeman, long before he was made a Sir, but even then he had an eccentric yet gentle manner which endeared him to almost everyone who met him. He was due to give our fifth-form class a talk about modern poetry, and after making as if to sit down in the elderly, very solid and unpadded oak chair provided, he smiled at us shyly and remarked with a wicked twinkle in his eye: "I think I'd rather stand!"

It was at about this time that a party of us went up to London to be given an official tour of the Houses of Parliament. Afterwards we were allowed a couple of hours to ourselves in London before having to catch the appointed train out of Victoria. I had already formulated plans for the occasion, and I and Nick Rose had arranged to meet up with Tim Foster, who had recently left Lancing and was now working for Radio Luxembourg. Tim had suggested that we meet him in his favourite venue, Studio 51, a jazz club in a basement just off the Charing Cross Road. This was my first visit to anywhere of this sort and I didn't really know anything about jazz at all at the time, but it was good to see Tim again. He recalls that there was a regular pianist and records were also played, so I suppose it was really the fifties equivalent of a disco.

In the 1954-55 school year there were only five of us in the sixth form specialist science class; this was presided over by Bill Dovell, who was also CO of the RAF section of the Cadet Force. The four others were Mike Steele (who now runs the family car dealership in Worthing), Howard Martin (college lecturer, artist and erstwhile trumpeter), Peter Keeling and David Barwell (about whose later years I have been able to find out nothing, regrettably).

Peter was a special friend and shared my interest in aeroplanes. I have already mentioned that he lived nearby in Worthing, and it was on a visit to his home that I first heard Frank Sinatra's "Songs for Swinging Lovers" and other seminal works.

One Saturday afternoon, the 2nd October 1954, I recognised a visiting aircraft, Hawk Trainer G-ALUX, as coming from Fair Oaks: this was painted in black and cream, a very distinctive colour scheme. I mounted my bike and got down to the aerodrome as quickly as I could (in about ten minutes) and, as bold as brass, walked out onto the airfield as the owner was returning to his aircraft. Mr William Way was an elderly man, and owned a large family business of builders' merchants in Wimbledon. He must have been sympathetic to my enthusiasm, and after a short conversation he asked me if I would like to go flying with him from Fair Oaks during the Christmas holidays. Would I just?! He was true to his word, and on the 27th December (which was Boxing Day that year) we flew together. That was my first Miles type, and remained the only one until 1996, when Tony Habgood took me up at Shoreham in the Messenger G-AKVZ.

When I arrived back at school at the end of January 1955, I noticed on my first visit to the airport that there were two new resident aircraft; one was the rare Miles Mercury G-AHAA, recently acquired by F.G. Miles Ltd, while the other was a Whitney Straight, G-AFGK; this had the incorrect registration G-AGFK painted under the port wing and I pointed this out to one of the hangar staff, but it was a at least couple of weeks before it was corrected.

Shortly afterwards I was asked by Bill Dovell if I would like to give a talk on aircraft to any school pupils who were interested. I did my research, some of it quite legitimately on Shoreham airport, and the great day, the 3rd March, dawned. Here, I thought, was my chance to indoctrinate some more potential spotters. But although, as might be expected, the attendance was far from phenomenal (well, a few did turn up), it was my introduction to public speaking, and I had to handle a slide projector too. Good experience, especially the bit about anticipating the size of an audience.

On the 18th March the Cadets had their 'big day out,' a visit to RAE Farnborough. This was a marvellous opportunity to log a lot of aircraft scattered around the airfield that the public could never see. A list of what I recorded on that day is given in Appendix 9.

A week later we were all taken to RNAS Ford, as we had been promised flights in Vampire Trainers. Of course, when the day dawned it was blowing pretty hard, and by the time we arrived at the airfield it had become so windy that all the promised trips had to be cancelled. Nevertheless we had a good snoop round all the hangars, and a list of what I saw is given in Appendix 5.

Shortly before I was due to take my GCE 'A' Level exams in June, there was an epidemic of glandular fever in the school; most of our small class – if not all – succumbed to this at the worst possible time, so that a week before the examinations we were lying in bed feeling pretty wretched. From the sanatorium I could hear various aircraft in the Shoreham circuit, and to keep my spirits up I kept a record in my diary of what I heard or saw, and then after I recovered I 'put the flesh on the bones' by interrogating friends and checking the aerodrome's Movements Books. But when the appointed time came for the exams I, along with several others, had to be gently coaxed into getting up and sitting the papers. Needless to say, we had not felt like doing any revision for the exams, and instead of passing in all three papers I had sat, I succeeded only in one (chemistry). That was to have a lasting effect on my plans for the next few years, as will be seen later. But in the shorter term I was due for a fascinating few weeks which I have never forgotten and which have had a profound effect on the whole of my life.

CHAPTER 5
THREE WEEKS IN THE LIFE . . .
(JULY 1955)

After 'A' Level examinations were over it was common for sixth-form pupils to get some work experience of one kind or another for the last few weeks of the summer term. Earlier that year I had given some thought to this prospect, and had resolved that I would somehow try to arrange something with F.G. Miles Ltd on the airport. However in practice this proved a lot more difficult to organise than I had thought; there was a lot of opposition at first to the idea, not from George Miles, who was most cooperative all the way through, but from both my parents and also the school's headmaster, who must have thought that I would be wasting my time instead of doing something they considered useful.

I still have two letters that were written on the subject to my father in early June 1955, which show that I must have been considered as something of a problem case! The first was from the headmaster, John Dancy (who was a classical scholar and had probably never met quite this situation before), and the second from my housemaster, Sam Jagger who, fortunately for me, was a pretty understanding sort of chap.

The first letter (from the headmaster) read as follows:

"Dear Mr Campbell,

Thank you for writing about your son. I am glad to see that you feel as I do about the matter in general.

We do not, as a matter of fact, normally allow boys to work outside the school, and I have told Peter that his case is not similar to that of other boys who are being allowed to go on courses of educational value, some of which are with industrial firms and others not. However, in view of his immense keenness for this subject I told him I would consider it as a special case, even though I do not myself share his tastes any more than you do.

I have now asked Mr Jagger if he will go down to see the Manager of the airport and ensure that Peter will be given work to do which is both sufficient and useful to himself and to the Aerodrome authorities. Provided that may be arranged I am prepared to allow him to go. I will see that you are informed when the final decision is taken.

Yours sincerely etc."

The follow-up (from my housemaster) read thus:

"Dear Mr Campbell,

I have today been down to see Mr Miles at Shoreham Airport. He and I have arranged that, with your permission, Peter will do three weeks in the Assembly Sheds there. This will entail a full six-day week from 8.30 to 5 and he will be the mate of a fitter on constructing aircraft there. He can have two days finally on the Coding Systems and the Landing Control of aircraft.

I have spoken to the Headmaster and he is now quite agreeable to Peter going there. Previously he was doubtful because he did not want him to slack about for three weeks after his 'A' Level exams and in this I quite agreed with him. I too am now in favour of the project.

Mr Miles is impressed with Peter and he should get a good report on him from his foreman after the three weeks; he says that he would be quite willing to recommend him to de Havillands for a place in the experimental and technical training establishment at Farnborough.

Kindest regards etc."

In the event I actually spent a whole week in Air Traffic Control, and all my lunchtime breaks during the next two weeks were also spent there! These weeks I remember with great pleasure and they were without doubt the most fulfilling of my young life up until then.

Shoreham had become quite busy by now. East Anglian Flying Services, who at the time flew between Ipswich, Rochester, Southend, Shoreham, Portsmouth, Paris (Le Bourget), Jersey and Guernsey, operated regular scheduled services (except in the winter months) with Dragon Rapides G-AEMH, G-AKJZ, G-AKRN & G-AKSC, and in 1955 were just starting to introduce Doves as well (G-ANVU, G-AOBZ & G-AOCE). The Southern Aero Club had two Tiger Moths (acquired from the Midland Flying Club at Elmdon), G-AKXO & G-ALVP, and two Hawk Trainers, G-AITS & G-AIZK. There were several other active resident aircraft including F.G. Miles Ltd's Gemini G-AKEL, H.B. Pursey's Gemini G-AJOJ, T. Carlyle's Messenger G-AIBD, E.W. Westbrook's Messenger G-AJDM and Meridian Airmaps' Autocrat G-AGXU and Aerovan G-AJKP.

A few years ago I learned from Philip Ansell (whom I had known since those early days when I used to meet him on the airfield occasionally) that all the old Aircraft Movements Books from Shoreham covering the 1950s were to be thrown out (quite unbelievable!), and fortunately I managed to acquire a selection of them. The oldest ones still in existence proved to date from the autumn of 1954 onwards, but that meant that the book covering July 1955, when I was working at Shoreham, should be amongst them. Imagine my feelings of nostalgia then, when opening up the book in question some forty years on, to find several pages of entries, all (or in part) in my (still recognisable) handwriting. Two of these pages (covering my first full day) are reproduced overleaf.

My first day working at Shoreham should have been Monday July 4th, but such was my keenness that I unofficially started on Sunday the 3rd. I was apprenticed to a vivacious red-haired lady air traffic controller (after racking my brains for some time I recall that her first name was Yvonne, and possibly her surname was Mitchell); she was very patient with her new charge, who wanted to be doing absolutely everything connected with ATC without any previous experience!

The first movement of that day was a placement flight in an East Anglian Dove by Capt. Whellem from Southend at 08.00, which then left for Guernsey with passengers at 08.33. Cecil Pashley checked the weather prospects in Hawk Trainer G-AIZK, and from then on the day became quite busy. Several Army Austers arrived for the start of a Summer Camp, which lasted some ten days, with a variety of aircraft coming and going during that period. Also Flt. Lt. Woods, a regular visitor, brought in Harvard KF729 from White Waltham, on this occasion staying overnight and leaving at 07.30 the next morning.

Mondays were usually very quiet as the Southern Aero Club did not operate on that day, but on this particular Monday, July the 4th, there was a wide selection of visiting aircraft – it was very hot and sunny. Unusual was the Anson G-ANWW of Fairey's, and there was also the first-ever visit of a new type, an Army Air Corps Auster AOP.9 from Middle Wallop, flown by Major Warburton – I remember marshalling the aircraft to the parking area and commenting as much to him as he exited the cockpit. The day also produced the inevitable crop of visitors from Croydon, and I well remember "Tiny" Marshall, one of the Surrey Aviation instructors, who was with a student on a cross-country flight. He was, as his nickname implied, a largish individual, and his being encased in the Sidcot suit obligatory for Tiger Moth flying all the year round made him look several sizes larger still. I can recall him complaining that his hayfever was really bad that day.

On Tuesday the 5th, two of the ubiquitous Aiglet Trainers operated by Airways Aero Associations paid a visit, and more service aircraft, both Chipmunks and Austers, joined the summer camp. On Wednesday the 6th, yet another Auster joined them and

UPPER: The unique Lycoming-engined Aerovan 6 G-AKHF, seen at Shoreham during the summer of 1953.
MIDDLE: B.A. Swallow 2 G-AFHS at Shoreham during the summer of 1953 (resident throughout the 1950's).
LOWER: Prince 3E G-AMLZ, a regular visitor to Shoreham during the mid-fifties.

UPPER: The Miles Sparrowjet at Shoreham during the late summer of 1953 (several months before its first flight).
MIDDLE: The Sparrowjet G-ADNL at Shoreham during spring 1954, with wheel spats removed.
LOWER: Yet another view of the Sparrowjet G-ADNL taken during 1954.

UPPER: A busy scene at the Shoreham Goodyear Trophy Meeting, held on the 28th August 1954, featuring the modified Gemini 1A G-AKKB and Mew Gull G-AEXF.
MIDDLE: More visitors to the Shoreham Goodyear Trophy Meeting on the 28th August 1954: the 'FLIGHT' Gemini 1A G-AKHC, Hawk Trainer G-AIDF and Avro Club Cadet G-ACHP in background.
LOWER: The Spartan Arrow G-ABWP with crew at Shoreham, 17th July 1955.

UPPER: Auster J/5K Aiglet Trainer G-AMYI at the Shoreham Goodyear Trophy Meeting on the 28th August 1954.
MIDDLE: Foreign visitor to Shoreham: Cessna 140 HB-CAV, seen on the 12th May 1955.
LOWER: The second Miles Aries G-AOGA after its first flight from Shoreham on the 23rd November 1955.

UPPER: 'FLIGHT' magazine's first Gemini 1A G-AFLT seen here in its original colours before acquiring a red, white & blue scheme. (Photograph by courtesy of 'FLIGHT' magazine and Quadrant Picture Library).
LOWER: The Hurel Dubois HD.31 F-WFKU seen at Shoreham during its press demonstration over the weekend of 27th & 28th March 1954. The small figure in the left background facing away from the camera is the author! (Photograph by courtesy of 'AEROPLANE' magazine and Quadrant Picture Library).

UPPER: The record-breaking Auster J/5F Aiglet Trainer G-AMOS with its owner Tom Hayhow at Fair Oaks, sometime during the summer of 1952.
LOWER: Lockheed 12A G-AGTL seen on one of its frequent visits to Fair Oaks from Croydon sometime during 1956.

UPPER: The Evening Standard's W/S S.51 Dragonfly G-ANAL at Croydon on the 18th July 1954, just before author's flight.
LOWER: Transair's Dakota 4 G-AMYW fitted with geophysical research equipment, seen here at Croydon on the 10th March 1956.

UPPER: Bonanza G-AOAM at Fair Oaks on the 31st July 1955, just before author's flight.
MIDDLE: Chrislea Super Ace G-AKUW seen here on the 18th September 1955 at its base at Fair Oaks, just before author's flight.
LOWER: Just one of hundreds, but a bit special all the same! A 'demobbed' Prentice at Stansted, seen on September 11th 1957, carrying the appropriate personalised registration of the author, G-APGC!

a Mr Barber (whom I shall refer to again later) flew in Dragon Rapide G-AHPU from Usworth for a stay of several days. An unusual visiting aircraft on Thursday the 7th was the Auster 5 G-AKOT from Denham. On Friday the 8th two individualized Hawk Trainers arrived, the red and spatted G-AIDF from Denham, and J.R. Johnston's coupé version, G-AJRT, from Fair Oaks.

On Saturday the 9th East Anglian were so busy that their Autocrat G-AGXP was pressed into service to ferry passengers between Shoreham and Portsmouth (can you imagine that being tolerated today?!). Mr Barber was due to fly his Rapide back to Usworth, but I remember him saying before he left that he didn't feel at all well. Nevertheless he took off on his long flight quite alone, and naturally we were somewhat concerned for him, although he had of course filed a flight plan. Later that afternoon we heard on the phone that he had had to make a forced landing at RAF Dishforth, after which he had collapsed at the controls; so he was really very fortunate still to be alive.

On Sunday the 10th, Capt. McDonnell, who had left for Le Bourget at 10.00 in EAFS Dove G-AOBZ, had to return shortly afterwards as one of the engines had had to be shut down in an emergency. This change of plan necessitated some quick thinking, but fortunately Dove G-AOCE had arrived from Jersey only two minutes before the emergency landing, so this was hastily turned round and eventually took over the Paris service only just over half an hour behind schedule – not bad going! But this technical problem and the resulting aircraft shortage had ramifications in all directions, and as a result the EAFS Proctor G-ANGM (something of a *rara avis*) was then used to ferry passengers in from Ipswich.

On Monday the 11th I began two weeks' work in the assembly hangars, and under the tuition of Bernie Fieldwick learned how to cut, drill and shape metal. I recall making amongst other things a couple of brackets to hold something or other onto the engines of the Aries G-AOGA, which was then nearing the final stages of construction. Also on that day Test Pilot Ian Forbes brought in Douglas Bader's Gemini G-AMGF from Croydon for a number of modifications to be carried out by F.G. Miles Ltd (which Ron Paine has discussed in more detail in *"Tails of the Fifties"*), and Mr Atherton paid one of his regular visits in Cub Coupé G-AFSZ from his strip near Dorking (at Ranmore Common, I believe). On Tuesday the 12th Mr Cooper's Hornet Moth G-AEET passed through en route from Le Havre to Southend.

Wednesday the 13th produced a marvellous sight early in the morning, namely four Ansons arriving in formation from Aston

3rd July 1955

INBOUND

Type of Flight	Type of Aircraft	Regis. Letters	Captain	From	A.T.D.	E.T.A.	A.T.A.
S	DOVE	G-ANVU	WHELLEM	SOUTHEND			0800
PC	MAGISTER	G-ATZK	PASHLEY	LOCAL			0925
S	DOVE	G-AOBZ	BURGESS	SOUTHEND			0930
PC	AUSTER	G-AGXP	WILLMOTT	PORTSMOUTH			1002
PC	MAGISTER	G-ATTS	PASHLEY	LOCAL			1013
PC	GEMINI	G-AKEL	BRUNICARDI	LOCAL			1025
M	AUSTER 6	VF581	CAPT HALL	HENLOW			1116
M	CHIPMUNK	WP905	CAPT DUNN	HENLOW			1117
PC	MAGISTER	G-ATZK	ATKINS	LOCAL			1118
S	DOVE	G-ANVU	WHELLEM	JERSEY			1119
PC	MAGISTER	G-ATTS	FRY	LOCAL			1121
PC	T.TOTH	G-ALVP	PASHLEY	LOCAL			1133
PC	GEMINI	G-AKEL	BRUNICARDI	LOCAL			1120
PC	MAGISTER	G-ATZK	SAILOR	LOCAL			1154
PC	TIGERMOTH	G-ALYP	WHEELE	LOCAL			1157
M	AUSTER 6	VX110	JONES	HUCKNALL			1239
PC	T.MOTH	G-ALVP	WHEELE	LOCAL			1240
PC	AUSTER	G-AGXP	WILLMOTT	PORTSMOUTH			1308
PC	T.MOTH	G-ALVP	WHEELE	LOCAL			1312
M	AUSTER 6	VF581	JONES	LOCAL			1320
S	DOVE	G-AOBZ	BURGESS	LE BOURGET			1359
PC	T.MOTH	G-ALVP	MOCKETT	LOCAL			1405
PC	GEMINI	G-AKEL	BRUNICARDI	LOCAL			1423
PC	MAGISTER	G-ATZK	PASHLEY	LOCAL			1440
M	HARVARD	KF729	F/L WOODS	WHITE WALTHAM			1500
PC	MAGISTER	G-ATZK	PASHLEY	LOCAL			1523
PC	T.MOTH	G-ALVP	WHEELE	LOCAL			1610
PC	GEMINI	G-AKEL	BRUNICARDI	LOCAL			1630
S	RAPIDE	G-AKRN	PASCOE	JERSEY			1638
PC	AUSTER 5	G-ANHS	HENRY	BEMBRIDGE			1720

3rd July 1955

OUTBOUND

Type of Flight	Type of Aircraft	Regis. Letters	Captain	TO ~~From~~	E.T.D.	A.T.D.	A.T.A.
S	DOVE	G-ANVU	WHELLEM	GUERNSEY		0833	
PC	MAGISTER	G-AIZK	PASHLEY	LOCAL		0920	
PC	GEMINI	G-AKEL	BRUNICARDI	LOCAL		1000	
S	DOVE	G-AOBZ	BURGESS	LE BOURGET		1007	
PC	MAGISTER	G-AIS	PASHLEY	LOCAL		1010	
PC	AUTOCRAT	G-AGXP	WILLMOTT	PORTSMOUTH		1016	
PC	MAGISTER	G-AITS	FRY	LOCAL		1040	
PC	T.MOTH	G-ALVP	PASHLEY	LOCAL		1042	
PC	MAGISTER	G-AIZK	ATKINS	LOCAL		1043	
S	DOVE	G-ANVU	WHELLEM	JERSEY		1142	
PC	GEMINI	G-AKEL	BRUNICARDI	LOCAL		1110	
PC	T.MOTH	G-ALVP	WHEELE	LOCAL		1110	
PC	MAGISTER	G-AIZK	SHAILER	LOCAL		1120	
PC	T.MOTH	G-ALVP	WHEELE	LOCAL		1212	
PC	T.MOTH	G-ALVP	WHEELE	LOCAL		1252	
M	AUSTER 6	VF-581	CAPT JONES	LOCAL		1314	
M	AUSTER 6	VX 110		LOCAL		1330	
PC	T.MOTH	G-ALVP	MOCKETT	LOCAL		1332	
PC	MAGISTER	G-AIZK	PASHLEY	LOCAL		1349	
PC	GEMINI	G-AKEL	BRUNICARDI	LOCAL		1405	
PC	AUTOCRAT	G-AGXP	WILLMOTT	BENBRIDGE		1440	
PC	MAGISTER	G-AIZK	PASHLEY	WHITE WALTHAM		1440	
S	DOVE	G-AOBZ	BURGESS	SOUTHEND		1455	
PC	GEMINI	G-AKEL	BRUNICARDI	LOCAL		1555	
PC	GEMINI	G-AKEL	BRUNICARDI	LOCAL		1623	
S	RAPIDE	G-AKRN	PASCOE	SOUTHEND		1653	

Down. I remember being at work in the assembly hangar and dashing outside to find out what all the noise was about. With another Anson arriving from Manston at lunchtime, this made an unforgettable sight of no less than five Ansons parked up together. Friday the 15th produced "Buster" Paine's famous red Proctor G-AHNA, which came in from Blackbushe and stayed over until the 17th.

That day also saw the arrival by road of Meteor FR.9 VZ608 for top-secret modifications. At the time I was obviously not aware of the nature of this work, but many years later in 1989, after I had met George Miles once again, he explained it in a personal letter to me as follows:

"The work on the Meteor originated with a contract from Rolls Royce who required a flying test-bed for the RB.108 engines which could cover the transitional flight range between vertical take-off and level flight with the lift engines shut down. The two RB.108s were installed on trunnions behind the cockpit with controls which provided several degrees of tilt in either direction from the vertical position.

Flight testing took place at Hucknall and provided data for the design of the Short SC.1."

So really this must have been the first beginnings of the project that finally culminated in the Harrier jump-jet many years later. Surprisingly, the Meteor VZ608 is still very much in existence, and is currently displayed at the Newark Air Museum following extensive refurbishment.

That weekend saw me back in ATC, quite voluntarily, after my first stint in the hangars, and Saturday the 16th produced a naval Dominie from Lee-on-Solent, NF871. Other visitors of note that day were Vivien Varcoe in his familiar Messenger G-AKKG, the Gemini G-AMME ferried in by Company Pilot Mr Brunicardi for minor work (and returning to Derby on the 18th), and Chipmunk WP861 from White Waltham with Flt. Lt. Woods; I remember being told at the time that this was the aircraft in which the Duke of Edinburgh had had lessons, but I have not seen this confirmed in other publications on the Chipmunk.

Sunday the 17th was another gorgeous day, and saw another fairly regular visitor, Dove G-AMFU from Leicester; we also had the first recorded visit by an aircraft unique both then and even today, the Spartan Arrow G-ABWP, which had been flown in from Denham. I remember going out to greet the crew, Mr Dennison and his lady companion, and they agreed to let me photograph them in front of the aircraft.

On Monday the 18th, Mr Pearse-Smith arrived in Auster 5 G-AJAK to carry out some banner-towing along the local beaches; this was a fairly regular occurrence during the summer months. On Wednesday the 20th the de Havilland Company's Beaver G-AMVU paid a visit from Hatfield, flown by Mr Lucas; George Miles, who always enjoyed the opportunity of adding new types to his logbook, took it up during the afternoon for a twenty-minute flight. Also on that day the Sparrowjet G-ADNL was flown up to Elmdon by Ian Forbes.

Friday the 22nd brought another regular visitor, Mr Martin's Prince G-AMLZ (normally based at Leicester but flown in on this occasion by a Mr Clark from Hendon), and another rarity, John Reid's DH.60 Moth G-AAWO from Tarrant Rushton. Saturday the 23rd saw Fox's Glacier Mints Rapide G-AIDL and Mr Challis' Aerovan G-AISF, inbound from its base at Eastleigh and outbound to Rhoose. Sunday the 24th brought another formation, this time of three Proctors from Croydon, led by the redoubtable Mike Conry in G-AKDZ (some of whose exploits were recounted by Eric Bell in *"Tails of the Fifties"*); the other two pilots were Messrs Speechly and McDonald in G-AIKJ and G-AKXK respectively.

The following day, Monday the 25th, was the last day of the school term, but looking through the Movements Book I see that I must have paid a final visit to the aerodrome, as my handwriting records the booking in of Hornet Moth G-ADKC from Eastleigh at 10.25! On reflection I think that this visit must have been primarily to see George Miles to thank him for allowing me to work on the airfield for the previous three weeks. I can remember that, although nothing had ever been said about my being paid, he presented me with a 'gift' of £6, not an inconsiderable sum in those days.

So ended three of the most enjoyable and unforgettable weeks of my life. When I met up with George Miles again a few years ago, he did actually remember me, which was not bad considering that almost forty years had passed and neither of us had got any younger!

So perhaps now is an appropriate time to say in my own small way: "Thank you, George!"

CHAPTER 6
ELEMENTS OF TRANSITION
(MID-1955–MID-1956)

This episode at Shoreham inspired me seriously to consider the aircraft industry as a career; I even bought a book called *"Chemistry and the Aeroplane"* in an attempt to justify the marrying of the two disciplines together. Although I did later have an interview with Sir Barnes Wallis at Vickers Armstrongs (Weybridge) with a view to becoming an apprentice, I eventually decided to carry on with the chemistry professionally and keep the aeroplanes as a hobby.

I cannot discuss this time period at Shoreham without recalling some fond memories of the Southern Aero Club's CFI, Cecil Pashley, and his wife Vera. Cecil was a small man with a big heart and a tall wife; he had learned to fly right back in 1908, and since then had amassed goodness knows how many thousands of hours in the air. Don Brown's book *"Miles Aircraft Since 1925,"* published in 1970 and now regrettably out of print, describes his part in the beginnings of F.G. Miles' aviation career. Cecil and Vera were based in the Southern Aero Club's wooden hut on the southern side of the aerodrome, and as a flying enthusiast I was always made very welcome. Vera made a lot of cakes for the fortification of the Club members, and she had a rather unusual way of disposing of the leftovers; a family of rabbits lived under the hut and became very partial to stale fruit cake and other titbits! Happily Cecil's part in the development of Shoreham Airport is now remembered for posterity by the naming of the airport perimeter road as Pashley Way on the 12th May 1991.

I have already explained that I had been ill with glandular fever just prior to the 'A' Level examinations in June, and had been coerced out of bed just to take them, so it was perhaps not altogether surprising that my results were unimpressive. It was agreed that I should return to school for one more term and then leave at the end of the year.

During the summer holidays, I enjoyed a memorable flight from Croydon on the 20th September 1955. This was classified as an Air Experience Flight, and to be eligible I had to be wearing my blue Cadet Force uniform; I was then entitled to about an hour and a half's worth of flying at Her Majesty's expense. A member of Surrey Aviation's Flying Group, Mr Hibberson, who had volunteered his services as pilot, met me at the airport and asked if there was anywhere I would particularly like to go; as it was a warm late summer day without a cloud in the sky, what else could I say but "How about Shoreham?" So we enjoyed an idyllic flight in the blue and yellow Hornet Moth G-AELO which, having side-by-side seating and a Y-shaped control column, made it possible for me to fly the aircraft for much of the time. When we arrived at Shoreham we had a cup of tea and I then telephoned my father to ask him to come and collect me at Fair Oaks; once back there safely I thanked the pilot for his kindness and left him to make the solo trip across South London back to Croydon.

In recent years I have had the privilege to get to know the current owner of G-AELO, Mark Miller, who has been extremely helpful with research I have been doing. Mark has his sights set on bigger things than Hornet Moths: he has nearly completed the rebuilding of Dragon Rapide G-AGJG which, many years ago when it was operated by Island Airways, used to provide joyrides from Heathrow!

The autumn term of 1955 proved to be rather an anticlimax in school itself, although I had been given certain responsibilities to discharge as a House Prefect. With no exams to prepare for, I spent a lot of time in the piano practice rooms. At the tender age of five some family friend had thoughtfully given me for Christmas the entire book of Beethoven's piano sonatas. Whether it was thought that I showed promise at that early age I have no idea, but I do know that the book was far more useful to me at that age if I sat on it!

I had for some years been trying to become more proficient on the piano (and latterly the violin, at which I failed miserably), and our teacher, John Alston, began to notice that, despite my practising, I seemed to be playing more by heart that by reading the music. My secret was out! He was absolutely right: I had always had a problem in trying to read two different staves at once with lots of black dots on them and so tried to memorise the music instead of following along in it. Mr Alston and I had a chat about this, and then he made a suggestion which was to prove pivotal as far as my future musical activities would be concerned.

He asked me if I would like to concentrate more on the theory of music, harmony and composition, to which I replied: "Yes, *please.*" Now here was something I could really get my teeth into. In a short while, instead of playing classical pieces very badly, I was composing my own songs. When at home I had been listening whenever possible to Radio Luxembourg's Top Twenty programme on a Sunday evening and knew well some of the hits by singers such as Dickie Valentine, Dennis Lotis, Alma Cogan and

Ruby Murray. The popular songs of the early fifties had fairly straightforward melodies, rhythms and lyrics (which one could easily follow), and I wanted to see if I could write my own. Later I hawked some of them round Tin Pan Alley in London but nothing ever came of it; not surprising, really, but I have been writing my own music and extemporising ever since those days! More of that later.

Meanwhile, my long-time friend David Timmis was having his own successes in this direction. David had always been interested in scientific subjects, particularly mathematics, and eventually developed a bent for engineering. But he was also fascinated by the arts, especially music, and became an accomplished player of both the accordion and the violin. In 1954 he and four of his schoolfriends had formed a dance band which they cleverly called "Five Got Rhythm," and they had played for several occasions, including the official school dance, which was attended by 'approved' young ladies from the local area (as discussed earlier). In 1955 they gave an excellent concert in the school hall for pupils and parents; this was the first time I had heard the then brand-new ballad "Young and Foolish," which became such a hit for Dean Martin and others the following year. I'm not quite sure how it happened, but David got a holiday job later that summer playing the accordion at Butlin's holiday camp in Filey. Somebody with influence must have heard him that night at Lancing....

David stayed on at Lancing until the end of the 1956 school year in July. During the summer term he flew in a Varsity to Chivenor and back on an ATC cadets' outing. But music was very much a going concern for him; an article in the London *"Evening Standard"* for May 15th 1956, headed "College Boy Band Plans a Tour," reported as follows:

"The 'Five Got Rhythm' dance band at Lancing College, Sussex – 18-year-old pupils – have decided to spend two weeks of the summer holidays touring the country.

They hope to raise a substantial sum towards the £120,000 college chapel building fund. The band was formed two years ago. It has had several public engagements already – spending the profits on music and instruments – and the boys' success encouraged them to plan the tour.

They are hoping that friends of the college will help arrange engagements."

Back in the autumn of 1955 there were plenty of other activities going on at Shoreham airport and in the Cadet Force to provide me with some needed spare-time interest. Apart from the first recorded visits of a Skeeter and a Twin Pioneer, and the first flight of the new Aries G-AOGA on the 23rd November (which is not the date usually quoted officially), several foreign-registered aircraft were noted; they included Messenger 2A EI-AHL (which became G-AIAJ early in 1956), Navion F-BESH, Auster 4 D-ELIT and TF-OSK, a Proctor 4. The Proctor was particularly interesting as it had been converted at Croydon directly from a demobbed RAF machine (NP278) and never carried a UK registration; it was intended for export to Iceland, but this never happened, and after a period at Croydon in early 1956 it eventually went to Sweden as SE-CDK in June of that year.

I have already mentioned that I had been made Flight Sergeant in the Air Force section of the Cadet Force earlier in the year. Now every fine Friday afternoon I was put in charge of assembling WZ796, the school's Slingsby Grasshopper primary glider, in one of the playing fields. The opportunity of a free, though short, flight was something that we all learned to wait for patiently week after week until, at last, it was our turn; being of senior rank, it was my duty to wait until all the other cadets had flown, but my turn eventually came on November 18th when I made my only solo flight – fortunately without incident.

For those readers unfamiliar with the aircraft (there are still a few in museums), it had a two-dimensional fuselage framework of spruce, with a plywood seat bolted on in front of a pylon which supported the wings with wire braces. Both the wings and tail unit were fabric-covered and fairly conventional. Before each flying session the glider had to be fully assembled, and then afterwards it had to be dismantled again for storage in a prefabricated concrete garage nearby.

When all pre-flight checks were complete, the aircraft was then attached to a stout peg that had been firmly driven into the ground. A V-shaped rubber bungee was fixed by a ring to the nose, and this was stretched to its extremes by two teams of 'volunteers.' Despite the vivid imagery that comes to mind of two teams of boys hurtling back towards the glider and converging at an ever-increasing rate, I am relieved to report that the launch was always uneventful in this respect. When a toggle was pulled by the pilot to release the glider, the acceleration was generally sufficient for the incumbent to leave the ground for ten or twenty yards; this was quite an experience to remember although it hardly compared with the first flight of the Wright Brothers.

Our only recorded mishap occurred when our Instructor, Bill Dovell, made a heavier-than-usual landing and his backside went right through the plywood seat! When I finally met him again in 1991, shortly before his retirement (he spent his entire career on the staff at Lancing) and reminded him of this occasion, he laughed and told me that he remembered it well! He then pulled out a photograph, which one of the boys had taken, of him actually airborne in the glider. Sadly Bill died of cancer within a year of this, shortly after retiring; he was a man truly dedicated to education in the broadest sense, and I will always be grateful to him for his advice and support.

I have recently learned that our erstwhile glider WZ796 is still in existence somewhere in Gloucestershire, owned by Peter Mallinson; I would love to sit in it again one day. There are few examples remaining now, but at the time Grasshoppers were standard issue to all schools with Air Cadet Forces.

And so on the 18th December 1955 I finally said my farewells to both Lancing College and Shoreham airport. Then from January until June 1956 I spent a very happy six months at Guildford Technical College preparing once again for the 'A' Levels.

Guildford Tech. was an eye-opener to me after the genuinely cloistered conditions at Lancing; here were a lot of young men and women in their late teens not just working together but socialising together too, and very successfully! How sensible the whole arrangement was, and how far my former school life now seemed to be removed from reality. This was a time when I worked hard, and yet had a real social life at last, meeting a wide variety of people, some of whom I like to think are still my friends today. It was during this period that I first met Ann Tilbury (who later worked as the librarian for *"Flight"* magazine, and was one of the few women ever to fly with the Red Arrows), Mike Jones (lifelong aircraft enthusiast and close friend), Mike Wilson (model-maker and glider pilot), David Grummett (business entrepreneur) and many others.

Despite the obvious attractions and distractions, this time I managed to get the necessary three 'A' Level passes, and opted to start a Chemistry Degree course at Sir John Cass College in London later that year.

CHAPTER 7
A DEGREE OF PROGRESS
(MID-1956–MID-1959)

In September 1956 I began studying at Sir John Cass College, London. At that time I was still living at home, so I came back to Woking each evening on the train from Waterloo. Travelling by rail had always appealed to me; now there were several challenges to be met so that valuable time was not unduly wasted on the daily journeys. The greatest of these was on a Thursday evening when we did not finish at College until 7.30 pm and the Goon Show, which was very much in vogue and not to be missed on any account, was broadcast at 8.30 pm.

Incidentally, I did attend two of the BBC recording sessions in London; these were, inevitably, even more anarchic than the broadcasts as the more outlandish sections of the recording were always cut before the public at large had a chance of hearing them. Nevertheless they contained nothing of any consequence compared to what passes for comedy entertainment today. For example, in a scene where a character got his head stuck in a falling sash window, Neddy Seagoon exclaimed "He's bleeding awful!": this the BBC cut as unsuitable.

It was always a close thing to get home before the broadcast, but my best recorded time from the College in Aldgate (in the City of London) to our home in Woking was just fifty minutes. This involved running from the College up Leadenhall Street to the Bank station, jumping on the next underground train to Waterloo (nicknamed "The Drain") and hurriedly scrambling onto the 7.50, first stop Woking. This was a Portsmouth-bound electric train of 1930s vintage, nicknamed the "Nelson" because of the configuration of the two windows at the front, the driver's resembling an open eye and the other being blanked off. These trains had a surprising turn of speed, and we rattled and swayed along the 24½ miles journey in as many minutes, sometimes reaching 80 mph, although it used to seem to me like 180! Then after a quick mile sprint on the trusty bike I was home just in time to tune in to Bluebottle, Eccles and Neddy Seagoon. I wonder how long it would take to do the same journey today.

How can I be sure that we reached 80 mph? Well, the traditional way was to count the time taken from one milepost to another, which gave you the mph figure with the minimum of calculation, but my ever-enterprising father had worked out a different method, which still works just as well today but only if you are travelling on the older track and not on the continuous welded rails which are now gradually replacing it. On the basis that each rail was 60 ft in length, all you had to do was to count the number of 'diddly-dums' in 41 seconds, and that was your speed in miles per hour. I did work this out from scratch for myself once (when I still knew how to do algebra!), and the method is quite correct.

On one occasion when I was in the usual hurry to get home, I came up the escalator at Waterloo to discover that the whole of the concourse was seized up solid with people. Trains were delayed and everything seemed to have come to a full stop. Only later did I discover that this was due to the arrival of an Americal 'star' with his band, Bill Hailey and the Comets. I suppose that I was of an age where I should have been wholeheartedly throwing myself into the spirit of this new phenomenon, but the whole episode left me strangely unmoved and I had a dislike of rock 'n' roll for many years afterwards!

However there was some entertainment more to my taste to be gained from travelling by the Underground, especially on the Circle line which I used daily. In 1958 there was a gigantic poster competition run by the *"Evening Standard"* which necessitated a great deal of vigilance during your travelling if you were to solve all the clues correctly. However, I managed to do this within the time constraints, and as a result was rewarded with four free theatre tickets, which I used to treat Ann Tilbury and Mike & Pat Jones to Julian Slade's "Salad Days" on my twenty-first birthday.

College was hard work but tremendous fun; by living at home I had the advantage of two social lives, and looking back on those three years I wish that today I had a fraction of the energy that I had then! At about this time I had become fascinated by geology, which I was studying as an ancillary subject in my chemistry degree course, and used to spend quite a bit of time during vacations scrambling around in the chalk quarries on the North Downs looking for fossils. I also joined an official College field trip to Westward Ho! in North Devon in the spring of 1957. Apart from performing some remarkable mountaineering feats on the massive tips at British Rail's quarries at Meldon, where some semi-precious stones were to be found, we had one glorious day when we walked all the way from Croyde Bay around Baggy Point to the southern end of Woolacombe beach, and then all the way along it to the northern end. This beach has remained one of my favourite spots to this day (but especially out of season). Unfortunately I was unable to get anywhere near RAF Chivenor, but I saw plenty of

Meteors, Hunters, Canberras, Varsities, and even a red Hawk Trainer and an Auster, which I have to assume were the North Devon Flying Club's G-AKAT and G-AJXC respectively.

One evening in 1958 the College put on some entertainment for the benefit of a charity, and as I was known to have pretensions to be a piano player, I was persuaded to do my bit. After announcing that I would play one of my own *de*compositions (this was, after all, a science-only College with a particular bias towards chemistry, so I hoped that the attempt at humour was not entirely lost on the audience), I tried them out with a piece in my latest *avant garde* style; this was intended to show that "It's not what you play, it's the way that you play it," because it involved just playing any notes and chords that my fingers happened to land on. But as I played this 'music' with plenty of expression, some listeners may have been deluded into thinking that I was genuinely influenced by someone like Schönberg. But this was an entirely free-form piece of abstract extemporisation and was not intended to be recognised as anything in particular – quite different to the playing of the late Les Dawson, for example, where you *knew* which tune he was playing, but it was played exquisitely *wrong* and using a technique which must have taken a long time to perfect: I know because I have tried to copy it! As Eric Morecambe once explained to André Previn (or André Preview, as he called him) on the Morecambe and Wise Show: "I'm playing all the right notes, but not necessarily in the right order!" Perhaps that concept applied in some way to my abstract music.

The strange thing was that this spoof went down quite well, and afterwards I was asked if I would like to play the piano (albeit in a more conventional style) to support the College's team entry in the London University Fashion Show being held at Queen Elizabeth College later that summer. As this was an all-girl establishment I did not need to be persuaded very hard!

The Students' Union and the College magazine *"Cassowary"* also took up a certain amount of our time. The slogan of one candidate in the Union elections was unforgettable: "Elect Ron, the current favourite." One of the students, Charlie Harness, became involved with the setting up of *"Private Eye"* magazine.

The editors of *"Cassowary"* were always ready and willing to publish original material submitted by the students. One longish article reflected the political views of the time in an 'exposé' of the private life of Pooh Bear.

I suppose I must have in some ways been a "bear of little brain" myself, because I found the language in many of the textbooks we were expected to use to be largely incomprehensible. As a tribute to all technical authors I therefore wrote a spoof extract from a highly technical but fictional work on biology, and submitted it for publication; it was accepted and read as follows:

THE DOLYCHOSPECTRADIX AND ITS PHRATOCRASM

"The bisporadic brachysmal dextraphon intrasagittated between the dosmic phlingible craton and the supratorial plentix is supertradulated bispondulaterally by the cross-tromed antiphrasm of the gringatron. Following the intradisprogation of a tripladicated sphorozal, a unicrandial process is inphlonicated whereby the spon- and nacro-newkatisms are destrilodally hemitronducated into the antiflugonactricalcyrotical state known to exist. Phractic research into the macrozyttal malcodomy of the systematic prophoritation encountered in this dinagolacteric reaction has undoubtedly shown that protocratyplasms, and not psychopneumoprods, are largely responsible for the dichonormadic specrodictulation noticed when hypernissal phormosiculists endeavour to intragulate the chronoschedillatory postaphedra."

[Extract from "Prophrastic Nodulisms of the Pronduphalia," Chapter Tron.]

A good exercise in proof-reading, maybe, but if I got it wrong, would anybody know – or care?

An anonymous contribution of verse in one issue appealed to me immediately; I thought I had kept a copy, but while researching this book I was unable to find it. It was so good that I have therefore taken the liberty of reproducing the parts I *can* remember (the beginning and the end) together with a new centre section, which maintains the flavour of the piece even if it is not identical to the original. The *denouement* is still the same, and that is the main thing.

So, with my apologies to the original author, whoever he (or she) was, here goes:

CRITICAL MASS

"There was a young boy called Frederick Werms,
Whose parents weren't on speaking terms,
So when he wrote to Santa Claus
It was in duplicate because
He asked his Dad and also Mum
For pieces of plutonium.
These both his parents, duty bound,
Individually found;
Providing for their offspring's leisure
Gave both of them the greatest pleasure.

Each crept into his room alone
And placed his presents, unbeknown,
Which came together in his stocking and
Laid waste ten square miles of land.
So learn from this dismal tale of fission
Not to mix science with superstition."

Another issue of *"Cassowary"* published a mock examination paper which I had written along with another student called Clive – initially for our own amusement; I am reproducing it in full here. Because much of the humour is typical of the times, it may have been dulled somewhat with age, but parts of it at least may still appeal to the scientifically-minded reader. It is worth bearing in mind that in those days some 'Practical' (i.e. experiment-based) Chemistry exams were up to seven hours in length, and were quite a drain both mentally and physically. On one vital occasion I managed to get a drop of a chemical in my eye (no protective glasses in those days) and lost a good half-hour. You were allowed to take in sandwiches and something to drink, though.

CRUNDON UNIVERSITY
CANDIDATES SHOULD NOT ATTEMPT MORE THAN 26 QUESTIONS
24 HOURS ALLOWED
(FOOD MAY NOT BE BROUGHT INTO THE EXAMINATION)

1. Given a thermometer (0-100°C) and a ladder, find the temperature of the sun.
2. Determine the velocity of water uphill.
3. Using the magnet and N/10 solution of Hydrochloric Acid provided, determine the air pollution in Camden Town.
4. Find 'g' by swinging on the light (compound pendulum).
5. Alternative method for finding 'g': jump off Beachy Head with a stopwatch.
6. Prove Archimedes' principle by sitting in a cold bath.
7. Determine the rate of leak of a water-cooled condenser.
8. Determine the maximum width of the Thames, using a metre rule.
9. Estimate the mean position of the travelling microscope.
10. Find the width of the room by swinging a cat around your head.
11. Using the cat (see Expt. 10) and an ebonite rod, find whether you are allergic to high potentials.
12. Evacuate the room.

13. Estimate the velocity of light, using the box of matches provided.
14. Alternative method using Einstein's equation: run backwards until you disappear and measure your velocity. This equals the velocity of light.
15. Determine the maximum value of 275, using the strings of beads.
16. By means of the given log of wood, find by integration the original height of the tree (assume Planck's constant).
17. Find Avogadro's number by counting.
18. By falling asleep on the given mattress, find its Time of Relaxation.
19. Pump up the tyres of a Carnot Cycle.
20. Prepare a pure sample of nitroglycerine, given 2 feet of copper wire, an iron bath, and sixpence in farthings. Record yield and flash point.
21. Suspend yourself under the given hydrogen balloon and determine the maximum distance at which the human voice is audible.
22. Fractionally distil the given mixture of cork and cardboard, and estimate the original percentage by weight of each constituent.
23. Using a triode amplifier circuit, knit yourself a leather walking stick.
24. Given one pair of German army boots, left, soldiers, for the use of, and a gravel pit, determine the coefficient of friction between leather and gravel at $20\,°C$.
25. Draw the Kelvin Family Tree and hence obtain Maxwell's Relations.
26. Tie the given brick around your neck and obtain a value for the terminal velocity of the human body in water.

Some of us experimented in the chemistry laboratories in a way which today would be considered to be inviting trouble, and probably was then; our sense of danger cannot have been too well developed at the time. Dave Walton and I became somewhat infamous for our interest in explosives and other novel effects. After trying with varying degrees of success to duplicate the effects produced by some indoor fireworks, I also attempted to make my own solid rocket fuel from sugar and sodium chlorate. After such foolhardiness I must be grateful still to be intact digit-wise, as otherwise playing the piano would now be even more of a problem than it is. Dave was even bolder; he instigated a 'controlled' experiment in a fume cupboard involving potassium permanganate and several other chemicals, which at its rather sudden conclusion succeeded in filling with acrid smoke the fume cupboards in all the other laboratories on different floors of the building.

For the benefit (or otherwise) of readers I will here divulge the formula for a 'smoke mixture' with which we used to surprise our friends (or lose them, or both):

Zinc dust	*36%*
Hexachloroethane	*44%*
Ammonium perchlorate	*10%*
Ammonium chloride	*10%*

I must say at this point that I accept no responsibility for this formula or its after-effects in any way, but I can assure you that it works – I'm mentioning it just so that you know I'm not kidding!

I then turned my mind to a somewhat less dangerous but just as flamboyant a pursuit; I decided to brighten up the fountains in Trafalgar Square. This had already been attempted by students of other colleges with standard water-soluble dyes, but I wanted to use the sodium salt of fluorescein, which gives a very intense and luminescent greenish-yellow colour even when very highly diluted, and which in artificial light would have looked spectacular. During one of our practical chemistry sessions we had all been given the task of preparing fluorescein, so by pooling all our yields I must have had several hundred grams of the stuff available as a deliquescent powder – quite enough to produce a spectacular effect, so I thought. One afternoon I prepared for my venture by dissolving the fluorescein in a concentrated sodium hydroxide solution (caustic soda), as the intense colour only develops under alkaline conditions. That evening I got on the tube train with two vials of the evil brown liquid in concentrated form and surreptitiously carried out the plan without incident; I hovered around rather nervously for a while afterward, only to find that nothing happened, absolutely nothing. Disaster! As a chemist, the likely reason should have dawned on me a lot earlier than it did; the colour only develops under alkaline conditions, so if the water was heavily chlorinated – which it almost certainly was – this would have made it sufficiently acid to render the fluorescein insoluble and hence colourless. Nice try, shame about the lack of forward thinking.

I'm a bit hazy about the reason behind a decision I took early in 1959. I know that I had recently taken rather a knock emotionally when a girl I was particularly keen on had told me that although she wanted to remain a friend, she had no intention of having any romantic attachment with me. Perhaps I had taken it harder than I should have, but I began to feel that it was my fault and that I must be lacking in some way. I wouldn't say I was suffering with depression but I needed something to happen to buck me up. Of course I realised later that experiences like mine were two-a-penny and all one really needed was to be able to discuss the problem with someone who had 'been there' before.

As you will have gathered, I used to be an avid reader of advertisements in the Underground, and at this time one in particular seemed to keep catching my eye: it recommended the Ramon H. Wings course to improve your self-confidence and overcome shyness. I therefore took the bull by the horns and went to a meeting to enrol, thereafter attending every Tuesday evening for about eight weeks.

After a week or two, the group of students got to know each other better and it turned out that many of the others on the course who were of a similar age (and single) had decided to attend for much the same reasons that I had! But we had paid out good money, and here were social skills and benefits we were being offered, so we willingly got ourselves involved. These skills were primarily concerned with improving the efficiency of our memories and gaining self-confidence by learning how to speak effectively in public.

The techniques for memory improvement were probably much the same then as they are today. To be able to remember lists of objects, tasks or people's names, we were encouraged to try and attach a mental picture to each item on the list, with some common linking factor if possible, so that the recalling of one item (and picture) would then recall to our mind the next one, and so on. It worked very well on the course, but even today I'm still hopeless at remembering the name of someone I've just been introduced to unless I'm given enough time to try and form one of these mental pictures!

As for speaking in public, first we were encouraged to go to the front of the class, stand on a small dais and read a printed passage out loud; this was to be repeated on the next occasion with a different passage until we became confident in doing it. (Reading in public was something I had not done since early in my school days.) The next phase involved our talking freely from the platform for just a couple of minutes about a particular subject we were familiar with. After that it became much more challenging: we had to talk about *ourselves*.

The final task on the course was the prior preparation of a short persuasive speech off a short-list of offered subjects, to last not more than about three minutes, the intention being for Mr W. to assess how effective we had become in influencing other people.

By now we were were all good friends, and even those who had been noticeably shy initially seemed to have few problems now in getting on with all the others. So Mr Ramon H. Wings, surprisingly enough, had for the most part succeeded in fulfilling his advertised promise.

What I learned on that course about speaking in public I have tried to put into practice ever since when I have been obliged to do this. But some are great orators, some are not. Perhaps, after all, it's a gift.

CHAPTER 8
MAINLY FAIR OAKS AND WISLEY
(1956–1960)

During my years at University between 1956 and 1960 I also spent quite a while at home studying, especially during the early summer before exams were due, and of course we enjoyed long breaks too between the terms. Our garden in Woking was an excellent place for plane-spotting. Apart from all sorts of local traffic movements, many airliners outbound from Heathrow passed almost overhead, including DC-3s, DC-4s, DC-6s, Vikings, Viscounts, Argonauts, Constellations and Stratocruisers. We were also right on the flight path between Dunsfold and Langley (Bucks), and sometimes the Hawker Company's aircraft would fly quite low overhead. These sported a midnight-blue colour scheme with gold trim, and the fleet included Hurricane G-AMAU, Anson G-AHXK, Dragon Rapide G-AHGC, Whitney Straight G-AEUJ, Tomtit G-AFTA and Cygnet G-EBMB.

At lunchtime on Sunday the 27th January 1957 I noticed a Stratocruiser, with nosewheel extended, circling very low in our vicinity over lunchtime; a news item on the radio later that day stated that this aircraft, carrying the Crown Prince of Iraq, had circled Heathrow for an hour and a half with a faulty undercarriage before eventually making a safe landing.

Also providing much excitement were the locally-built Valiants and Viscounts (and Scimitars, which were produced at South Marston) being test-flown from Wisley; they regularly made circuit after circuit at very low level, often disappearing from my view behind the trees. I also witnessed the first flight of the Vanguard on the 20th February 1959, and was at the end of the runway at Brooklands when the first VC.10 took off at about half past five in the afternoon of the 29th June 1962!

Although I have to admit that I enjoyed watching these aircraft from a relatively safe distance, life for those living directly beneath their flight path must have been unbearable, and such low flying over built-up areas would never be tolerated today. I logged almost every Valiant built, including the all-black WJ954, and also a wide variety of British- and foreign-registered Viscounts. I did make occasional visits to Wisley airfield itself, but it was not easy to see very much because of buildings and trees. However I do remember that Vickers operated a B-50 Washington WW349 and the Wellington MF628 for a time, as well as Canberra WD935 (which on one occasion overshot the runway and blocked the main road).

Other company 'hacks' included Dragon Rapides G-AHJA and G-AHKB, Dove G-AKSV and Herons G-ANNO and G-AOGW. A great variety of unusual aircraft visited Wisley during the fifties, although I cannot have seen more than a fraction of them.

Whilst recuperating from a tonsillectomy in August 1957 I somehow managed to get on an official trip round the Viscount production line at Weybridge; no less than thirteen of them were in various stages of completion.

Earlier I mentioned that I made small model aircraft, but my interest had by now extended to free-flight diesel models too, powered by such famous engines as the 1 cc ED "Bee," the 1.46 cc ED "Hornet" and the Allen-Mills AM.10 "Mercury," which was a remarkably powerful engine for its size, weight and capacity. I also built and flew aircraft powered by Jetex solid-fuel rocket engines; these were great fun, probably because they were slightly unpredictable, although generally they worked very well. The fuel was a brown cylindrical pellet (about ¾ in by ½ in) which you slid into an aluminium combustion chamber. You then coiled up half of a three-inch piece of brown fuse wire and sat the coiled end in contact with the pellet, holding it firmly in place with a gauze disc pressed down onto it. The lid of the combustion chamber contained a small hole for the fuse (and later, the jet exhaust gases) to pass through, and when you were satisfied that this was completely clear you fitted it to the body of the motor with retaining springs, making sure that about a ¼ inch of fuse was left proud of the hole. The motor was then clipped onto the underside of the model, which was protected from prematurely catching alight by strategically-placed asbestos sheeting. It was then a case of lighting the fuse, waiting until the fuel pellet ignited, and once it was developing full thrust you launched the model. After that, anything could happen. I recently saw one of these Jetex motors on display at the Southampton Hall of Aviation – it was really quite technically advanced for the modeller of the fifties.

Before I had passed my driving test in September 1955 I had designed and built a carrier for these models, to be strapped on my back whilst cycling, and this proved very successful. All free-flight models were flown on Chobham Common, a vast tract of heather-covered land at one time used by the military. I lost for good one model, which even after the motor cut continued to soar on thermals until it went out of sight. Although my name and address was on it, I never heard anything more of it. Today the M3 runs through the northern edge of the common just by what we used to call Chobham Clumps, a small group of weather-beaten fir trees.

My aeromodelling was encouraged further as my father, who used to visit Yugoslavia regularly on business, had a friend over there whose son, Dragan St. Hristic, was the champion aeromodeller of the country, and we used to exchange ideas regularly.

Many aircraft from Fair Oaks used to overfly Chobham Common, and I usually made a detour to the aerodrome on my way home. I also made other regular visits; I got to know the Air Traffic Control staff quite well, and was therefore allowed (for five years or more) to abstract whatever information I wanted from the Movements Books.

Just to try and clear up one etymological point: should the name of the airfield be two words or one? Although *"Aeroplane"* referred to it in 1937 as "Fairoaks," it was known locally throughout the second World War and afterwards as "Fair Oaks," despite Ambrose Barber telling me that his 1944 wartime standard flying map (¼ in to 1 mile) has it marked as "Fairoaks"! The two-word form was certainly in use during throughout the fifties to my knowledge, and exactly when the use of one word was restarted in earnest is not certain, but Mike Jones suggests it could have been during the sixties when Doug Arnold, the then owner, called it "Fairoaks Airport." Mike also tells me that the original name of the area could have been "Four Oaks" until the landowner cut down the eponymous trees when creating the airfield in the thirties.

Thanks to various contacts I had made, mainly through my school friend Tim Foster, I was fortunate to fly in quite a variety of light aircraft, generally from Fair Oaks (see Appendix 16). Tim was by now a member of the Experimental Flying Group at Croydon, and seemed to know and be known by almost everybody. One day he arranged for us to be flown from Fair Oaks by Colonel Fox, the owner of Super Ace G-AKUW; the visibility from the cabin was superb, and I was able to take quite a reasonable photograph of Windsor Castle as we flew over en route to White Waltham. On another occasion, Tim arrived at Fair Oaks in one of the Group's Hawk Trainers (G-AITN) to meet Len Snook, owner of Bonanza G-AOAM. Tim had always had a 'thing' about Bonanzas: back in 1953 he had persuaded our Physics teacher at Lancing, Mr Wigg, to drive us down to the airfield at Shoreham at very short notice when a Swiss-registered example had flown in (HB-EGB). On this occasion he used his same charms on Len, who kindly gave us both a short flight, my first experience of a V-tail!

The local flying Club, operated by Universal Flying Services, then had a number of 'demobbed' Tiger Moths, and also a couple of Austers, G-AIGU & G-AJDV. 'JDV had been on strength for a number of years, but 'IGU had been acquired early in 1955 after the previous Auster G-AHSO had suffered the ignominy of losing its propeller in flight and then making a forced landing; it had subsequently gone to Mitchells at Portsmouth and was rebuilt as a J/1N Alpha. That year the Club had also civilianised two ex-RAF Chipmunks, G-AORK & G-AORL, named 'Klondyke Kate' and 'Diamond Lil.'

David Timmis had come to Lancing as a pupil a year after me; we still shared the same love of aeroplanes and he often came with me on my sorties. Early in 1957 he was awarded a Flying Scholarship, and obtained his PPL at Fair Oaks in record time, less than a month.

David's son Alexander has very kindly allowed me to borrow his Log Books, which record that his first lesson was in Tiger Moth G-ANUD on the 8th April 1957 with the instructor Ted Cobbett. He flew intensively during the University vacation period over the next few weeks, and on the 3rd May he achieved his goal when Wing Commander Arthur passed him out in Tiger Moth G-AODV; his PPL course had taken just 26 days and exactly 40 hours flying.

After this achievement I was always welcome to fly with him during his time down from University, especially if I was prepared to contribute towards the cost of hiring the plane. Tiger Moths available for hire at £3-7s-6d (£3.37) an hour were still very much *à la mode* transport in those days for the serious aviator.

On the 24th July, less than three months after David had got his licence, we decided to embark on a cross-country to Shoreham; the aircraft was G-ANUD, in which he had had his first lesson. About ten minutes or so after passing Guildford, we spotted ahead the tell-tale plume of smoke from the cement works just south of Steyning (sadly no longer there to act as a giant warning windsock to visiting pilots), and within a few minutes landed at Shoreham, just after 15.30 local time. We had a cup of tea and then examined the visiting and resident aircraft, which included the HDM.105 Aerovan-based development (G-AHDM) and the Miles Student, still in its Class 'B' markings as G-35-4.

Within about an hour we took off for Fair Oaks. The weather that afternoon was beginning to deteriorate from the south-west; the sun had gone in and the cloud, although still fairly high, was developing a lower layer which could only bring rain in time. There was not much communication between us (those Gosport tubes were not intended for casual chat), but after about twenty minutes I realised that, whereas we should have been somewhere near Guildford, I was unable to recognise any of the terrain beneath us.

I was not made to feel any more confident when I yelled as much down the tube to David and he too admitted that he didn't recognise where we were!

So there we were, two inexperienced teenage aviators, in charge of one of the Club's Tiger Moths, without radio, in rapidly worsening weather conditions, and without being too sure of just how much fuel there was left (this last was fairly usual in a Tiger). I can't say that ours was a unique situation, but it is not one that I can recommend in any way; in fact, I think that if it was to happen to me now it would prove to be a real 'change of underwear' experience. But oh! for the innocence and optimism of youth! At the time we had probably never tasted real danger before, so can't have recognised the true potential of the situation. Quite undaunted, we decided to press on, hoping to identify some feature or other, and it was not too long before we came upon a railway line (inevitable in those days). We followed it northwards until we spotted a station, and then with one of David's famous side-slips we quickly lost enough height for me to be able to recognise it as Haselmere (on the main line from Waterloo to Portsmouth and about halfway between Fair Oaks and Portsmouth); we were at least 25 miles further to the south-west than we should have been! All I can think of is that David must have set up the compass incorrectly before we left Shoreham, but we certainly much appreciated the opportunity to fly by 'Bradshaw' that day, and reached Fair Oaks in the rain but without further incident in another twenty minutes or so. We were closely followed in by J.R. Johnston's Hawk Trainer Coupé, G-AJRT, which had left Shoreham three-quarters of an hour later than us!

It has come to my mind more than once since then that perhaps it was that particular experience which made David realise that he had a lot to learn in the navigation department: he certainly made up for it later.

We flew together on several occasions after that without incident. Then, with both David and myself working for a living, and with him being in Derby at Rolls Royce and me still in Surrey, we tended not to see very much of one another, although I knew that he had become very involved with the Tiger Club. Lewis Benjamin remembers him in particular for his audacity in planning a foray above the Arctic Circle in the Arrow Active G-ABVE (of which he was part-owner at the time); this aircraft was – and is – not the easiest to fly, and after a slight accident on landing on a tarmac runway the trip was unfortunately not completed. Later David also became known for his navigation skills; he was at one time Captain of the British Precision Flying Team, and he would occasionally take part in races such as the King's Cup as well.

Fairoaks (note the modern spelling on this occasion) is another aerodrome, like Shoreham, that was perhaps more charismatic in the fifties than it is today. The CFI was Wing Commander Arthur (mentioned earlier), who apart from his prewar and wartime exploits was remembered at that time for his stunt-flying in Tiger Moth G-AHRM for the film "The Sound Barrier" (although I should hasten perhaps to add that this particular aircraft was incapable of more than about Mach 0·15).

Even in those days airfields used to receive complaint calls from local residents irate about something or other. On one occasion an elderly lady telephoned complaining about the noise emanating from the airfield and insisting that he stopped his large jet bombers from flying over her house; he patiently explained that it was Wisley she ought to be phoning. On another day, all activity around the Control Tower ceased for a while as a huge cloud of bees came across the airfield and decided to swarm on the flagstaff fixed to the side of the building. A local expert was eventually found to take them away safely and operations resumed.

Another flying Club based at Fair Oaks had what must be the longest name of any Club, The London Transport Central Road Services Sports Association Flying Club; they operated the red and silver Tiger Moths G-AIIZ, G-AIJA and G-AKGF, and later also the Alpha G-AJAC. The Club is still very much in existence today.

"Flight" magazine's Gemini G-AFLT was based at Fair Oaks during the early fifties, and when it crashed at Merrow near Guildford on the 10th January 1954 the remains were brought back to the airfield, and I still possess small sections of ply and fabric which I retrieved from the wreckage, in the well-known red, white and blue livery. "Flight" then purchased a replacement Gemini, G-AKHC, which became just as well-known on the display scene as its predecessor. From 1956 the Automobile Association also based their aircraft at Fair Oaks, an Auster Alpine appropriately registered G-APAA; this was finished in a garish yellow and black scheme which may have been suitable for the AA's road vehicles but did nothing for an aircraft; the Alpine was replaced later by a Dragon Rapide G-AHKV in the same yellow 'livery' (I choose the word carefully.).

Various well-known people frequented the aerodrome throughout the decade. The record-breaking Tom Hayhow hangared his Aiglet Trainer G-AMOS there; regrettably he lost his life in an accident in Bavaria on the 10th April 1953 while attempting to set a new record time to Yugoslavia. Mike Hawthorne the racing driver flew a Fairchild Argus (G-AJSH) from there and, later, a Vega Gull (G-AHET); he too was to die, this time in a car accident on the Guildford bypass.

In the late fifties the comedian Dick Emery was much in evidence at Fair Oaks. He had developed a passion for flying to the extent that he preferred to be known as a pilot rather than a comedian; nevertheless he often provided some impromptu entertainment by putting on some of the voices and mannerisms for which he had become famous (such as "Ooh, you are awful!"). He flew in Club aircraft for some time and only purchased his own aircraft, the ex-Experimental Flying Group's Hawk Trainer G-AITN, in 1961; this was withdrawn from use late in 1962 when the C. of A. expired. He acquired the Tiger Moth G-AOEL, and then exchanged it for another one purchased from the local Club, G-ANDV; this he eventually wrote off at the Royal Aeronautical Society's Garden Party at Wisley in 1966 when the engine failed after take-off. In the ensuing forced landing the undercarriage took the roof off a Morris 1000 Traveller. Fortunately no one was hurt as a result.

Other well-known figures to be seen occasionally included Peter Masefield, who flew a modified Chipmunk, and Lord Trefgarne, who later flew a DH Dragonfly back from the antipodes. And then of course, there was the indefatigable Norman Jones, the founder of the Tiger Club; over the years quite a few of the Club aircraft were hangared at Fair Oaks and there was always an annual display there from 1958 onwards. I have included some details of the Tiger Club's aircraft at that time in Appendices 14 & 15.

I think it was Ann Tilbury who first suggested that I join the Young Conservatives (YCs). Ann and I had first met at Guildford Technical College; she tells me that I was very shy in those days, and that David Timmis (whom we had both known for most of our lives) had suggested that as a way of getting over my shyness I should strike up a conversation with her at the bus stop one day. I must have done just that, as we are still on speaking terms today!

I 'signed up' with the YCs in 1956, not out of any real interest in things political (even today, neither the middle-ground nor the extreme parties ever seem to be able to fulfil the grand promises always made just prior to an election) but mainly because of the large range of social activities; far more importantly, it was a marvellous opportunity to make friends and, above all, to meet *girls*. I am sure that this was the *main* reason because in 1964, immediately I started going out with Honor, the girl who was to become my future wife, I stopped attending – better things to do!

Apart from local meetings where we listened to talks and discussed all matter of subjects in earnest, there were social events too such as car treasure hunts, dances and visits to places of interest, so of course it wasn't long before a trip was organised to Fair Oaks! I will not mention who was responsible for this, but you may make a guess.

Another good friend I made at the time was Alex Mair. I recall that her father, who habitually wore a black beret for some reason, had the very rare skill of being able to play, very professionally, the musical saw. Alex and I were out for a drive on the 18th August 1958 when we happened to pass by some large black sheds (maybe they had been hangars once) near West Byfleet in which, unbeknown to me, part of the Science Museum's collection of aircraft had been stored. Now they were to be moved, and there sitting outside in one piece and on its undercarriage was the Handley Page Gugnunc, G-AACN!

Ann Tilbury recalled her memories in *"Tails of the Fifties"*:

My enthusiasm in flying was whetted when a club to which I belonged organised a visit to our local airfield, Fair Oaks, just to have a look round. I was particularly intrigued as my mother had worked there during the war and "WingCo" Arthur, who had known her at that time, was still working there as the Club's CFI.

It was during that period that I started work on "Flight" but that was almost by accident. I replied to an advertisement which merely stated that the vacancy to be filled was on a magazine, and it was not until I was told that I had the job that I was informed it was on "Flight" – did I happen to know anything about aircraft? So I cited my mother's wartime job (which was secretarial, with the ROC) and the fact that my cousin had done his National Service in the RAF. That, and the fact that I lived just about under the Fair Oaks circuit and could therefore recognise a Tiger Moth, known locally as a "Chobham Chaser," was the sum of my knowledge of aviation at that time. I stayed with "Flight" for some seventeen years!

Ann got to know a lot of aviation personalities over the years and, apart from flying with people such as Bill Cobbett (her first flight, in his Aeronca 100 G-AETG), Henry Pelham, Mark Lambert, Humphrey Wynn, Harald Penrose, Neville Browning and Brian Lecomber, she was in fact one of very few women to fly with the Red Arrows. She has also maintained her friendship over the years with two other well-known figures, Arthur Ord-Hume and the ex-Auster chief test pilot and Chilton expert Ranald Porteous, who died in 1998; it was through her introduction to them both that I was able to encourage them to write chapters for our recent book *"More Tails of the Fifties."*

1958 saw regular night-flying at Fair Oaks, generally on a Wednesday evening, and sometimes until half-past ten at night. My diary reminds me that Saturday 7th June was officially termed by the media "Flying Saucer Day." I know I didn't see any myself, but if there were a few strange lights in the night sky over Woking, they were more likely to be caused by Tiger Moths than by aliens.

I cannot let this occasion pass without recalling perhaps the most unusual character to frequent Fair Oaks, although this was later, in 1962. My own memories are aided by re-reading a short article from Air-Britain's *"British Civil Aviation News"* that was obviously written (using the details I provided) by someone with a far better turn of phrase than myself – probably Bernard Martin!

It seems that a certain Mr W.L. Manuel of Chertsey built over the period of about seven months an ornithopter he called 'Skybike'; this comprised an conventional, if elderly, bicycle fitted with lightweight wheels, 25 ft span wings of sharp dihedral, and a box fuselage supporting an all-flying tail. It had an overall length of 15 ft and an empty weight of 130 lb (with tyres inflated); manually propelled by Mr Manuel and a 4 ft propeller, it was hoped that the downhill slope at Fair Oaks would help him get airborne but I only ever saw him manage to raise the front wheel off the ground whilst pedalling and flapping the wings simultaneously.

CHAPTER 9
MUSICAL NOTES
(1956 ONWARDS)

During the second half of the fifties I also began trying to develop my musical skills further. Various friends I had made among the YCs were also musical: Mike Creevy had a good singing voice, Richard White played the drums (or more accurately a snare drum) and Alistair McKay was a clarinettist. We therefore formed a cabaret act as "The Four Friends" (very original). The four frequently became five when we included an extremely good-looking girl, Cindy Kilshaw, who sang in the Judy Garland mode; later she became a model. I was very much into the music of Tom Lehrer at the time, which we used to perform, along with some of my original compositions; I still have a tape of Mike singing some of my original songs. Richard's *forte* was a spirited vocal rendition of "Bueno Sera."

When we started being offered engagements, I began to think more seriously about the possibilities of earning some money from my music (at the time I was still at College and needed to supplement my allowance). In the spring of 1959 I saw an advertisement in the local paper advertising for a pianist for modern jazz sessions which were being held weekly at the Labour Hall in Woking. Despite the fact that I knew nothing of modern jazz I turned up one evening and was given the opportunity to sit in with the band.

My problem was that over the years I had developed a Charlie Kunz style of playing that was well-suited to playing solo pieces but was completely at odds with any form of music that was intended to 'swing.' In fact, I had no idea how to 'swing,' not even knowing what the term meant. Initially I assumed that it must be just another style of playing I needed to learn, but soon found out that there was much more to it than that – it was an approach to music that you had to feel from within to be able to do it successfully: you couldn't necessarily learn how to, and some people apparently never did. As can be imagined, after the session I felt extremely embarrassed as I was sure that I must have spoiled in no uncertain way everyone's musical pleasure that evening.

In fact there is a simple test which determines whether people understand the feeling of music that 'swings.' Here I must be careful with my words for 'swing' has had a number of different meanings over the years; I am referring to the sort of music that was played by the Ted Heath band, the Nelson Riddle orchestra with Frank Sinatra, the pianist Oscar Peterson and so on. If you hear audiences clapping in time to music, as they sometimes do, you will find that almost all of them spontaneously clap on the first and third beats of the bar: this kills the rhythm of the music stone-dead. It is very rare to hear anyone clapping on the second and fourth beats of the bar, but if they do they are showing a natural rhythmical feeling which reveals that they understand music that 'swings.' Try it yourself, or watch a TV audience, and you'll soon understand what I mean.

I can still recall some of those present on that occasion: there was Tony Lambden, the drummer, who was an actor and also owned an Austin 8, a car I took a liking to, eventually acquiring my own some ten years later; and Alan Smith, who was the organiser and electrical genius. The saxophone player, John Renshaw, took me in hand and we became good friends. I was still living at home, but John had his own bungalow where we could practise without upsetting the neighbours, and over a period of several years I was welcomed to his home almost every Sunday morning. There he encouraged me to listen to modern jazz records and to try and gradually modify my style of playing. As I was used to playing largely by ear anyway, modern jazz soon began to appeal more to me, although it took several years before I considered myself at all proficient in playing it. I recall that I started going to concerts at the Fairfield Halls at Croydon, where Norman Granz used to present the very best of American entertainers. Amongst others I saw were the Stan Kenton band, Ella Fitzgerald, Erroll Garner and Oscar Peterson (who became my role model – if I could play a tenth as well as him I'd be a happy man. So sad that he has had a stroke in recent years). Jazz from the late fifties and early sixties (or jazz in that style) remains my favourite sort of music today.

In 1960 I began getting more regular music work, first as part of a trio with drummer Tom Matthews and double bass player Peter Marks, then later with Mick Barney on vibes, when we called ourselves "The Riverside Quartet"; with varying personnel (the quartet later comprising Malcolm Potter, Bert Shipp, Brian Copping and myself), we played on right through the sixties. We covered quite an area, anywhere within about fifty miles of Woking, which meant that frequently we were in London until the early hours. I remember Bert Shipp, the bass player, who was the sales manager for a local garage, once remarking to me that I was the only driver he knew that he could trust enough during late-night journeys for him to go to sleep in the passenger seat – a compliment indeed. Little did he know how difficult it was for me to keep awake in the driver's seat sometimes.

The way that musicians were treated by hotel staff varied a great deal, but often it seemed as if we were being considered as a lower form of life. I can recall one New Year's Eve at a large and prestigious London hotel when, during the break, we were taken through into the kitchens for something to eat. By this time I was working for the Milk Marketing Board and was beginning to know something about food and hygiene and I was, frankly, far from happy – if only the paying guests had been aware of the conditions they would have probably packed up and left straight away. What we were offered was sandwiches, which was fair enough, but what I noticed was that whatever they had been spread with was clinging like crazy to the roof of my mouth – a very unpleasant experience, making it difficult to swallow. It was several years later when I became involved with the technicalities of pastry-making that it dawned on me that these sandwiches must have been spread with what is termed pastry margarine; this is intentionally a high melting point fat and is used to provide lift to puff pastry. You would have thought that the minion responsible would have realised what he was using as it could hardly be called spreadable. I've always been wary of classy hotels since then.

The Crown pub at Chertsey was a regular meeting place for jazz enthusiasts on a Tuesday night, and you could always sit in for a while. Also the Midas Club in Woking opened up at the end of 1960, and here we used to be treated to the very best in jazz on Sunday evenings. Later on I used to go to a pub at Hampton Court where professional groups such as the great Tubby Hayes quartet used to play occasionally. Tubby was a virtuoso on many instruments including saxophones, vibes, flute and piano, and his early death in 1973 was an incalculable loss to the British jazz scene.

Tom, Peter and I used to travel everywhere in my Austin A40 Farina – this must have been about 1962; the bass went on the roof rack, and Tom's drum kit, my electric piano and the three of us somehow used to all fit inside. I had purchased this Höhner piano from the accordion specialists, Bells of Surbiton; it turned out to be the first one they had sold in the country, and consequently I had plenty of teething troubles with it. It replaced an accordion that had been my stand-by instrument for a while. Pianos in local halls, clubs or hotels were almost inevitably ignored, as far as upkeep was concerned, until suddenly they were needed for a function. They were often a piano tuner's nightmare, as not only would some of the notes not work at all, but they would be suffering with damp (both water and beer), and were almost inevitably flat in pitch. Earlier I had become so frustrated at this that a friend had made me a piano-tuning key. On one occasion, in a large hall in Woking, I had had to tune two octaves of the piano before the quartet could play; this was an impossible situation – hence the accordion and then the electric piano. Later I used one of the first portable electric organs, an "Ace Tone" from Japan which I purchased from the Arthur Lord Organ Studios in Woking (the name was perhaps appropriate for a chemist!). It was certainly good to be free of the constraints of 'duff' pianos at last.

Tom worked for Elton's, the local office supply company, and Peter had a factory job at James Walker and Sons, who manufactured gaskets and jointing compounds for the automotive and other industries. I thought he really deserved better, but he used to remind me that the repetitive nature of the job made it possible for him to do other things in his mind at the same time, such as practising the double bass or flute (which he also played very proficiently). The factory was known as "The Lion Works," and when people asked Peter what he did at "The Lion Works" he would tell them that he put on the ears.

Peter was very creative in matters of comedy, and he and I used to tape-record comedy routines just for our own amusement under the general heading of "Two Grades of Pete." We also recorded an original musical composition of his, which he had entitled "Sponphony No. 1"; this *magnum opus* was in four movements, Allegro, Andante, Axolotl and Escrediadeddl, and required us to use not only all the different musical instruments that came to hand (such as double bass, harmonica, accordion, flute, miniature xylophone and penny whistle) but also a variety of potentially noisy domestic bits and pieces such as the coal scuttle, poker, fire guard, egg whisk, cardboard boxes, saucepan lids, cutlery (strung up on a line and struck with a stick to make them jingle) and all their baby daughter's squeaky toys. We recorded this in sections over a number of weeks and I still have a copy today, although the sound quality is pretty awful. Anyone know if and where I can get it 'restored'?

During the early sixties I organised a series of "Jazz Balls" each January at the Newlands Corner Hotel near Guildford. These were always very well attended, despite problems with the weather at that time of year, and we used to have three or four bands or groups to perform in sessions during the evening. One year we managed to get the well-known lady saxophonist Kathy Stobart and her husband, trumpeter Bert Courtley, to be the star guests for the evening. Kathy is still active in jazz today down in Devon.

For several years into the early sixties Peter Marks and I also collaborated on projects for the Witley Pantomime Company. This was a very talented amateur company amongst whom I made many friends. Peter wrote the script and I arranged the music. Our trio then played for the public performances each January. I am still in contact with Jean and "Chalky" White from those happy days.

My interest in jazz and other musical entertainment has continued, and despite a hiatus from 1971 for nearly twenty years when the demands of my work precluded my taking on any public engagements, I am now, in semi-retirement, as busy as ever and still enjoying the challenge. Old pianists never die – they just lose their keys.

CHAPTER 10
TRANSPORTS OF DELIGHT
(1955 ONWARDS)

I began to learn to drive just as soon as I was legally able, during the 1955 summer holidays, and fortunately passed my test first time in September. By then my father had recently parted, after many years, with a wonderful old 1930 Austin Six saloon PL 3199, in which he gave me a few preliminary lessons (the 'Six' referred to the number of cylinders, not the horsepower as with the Austin Seven; I believe it developed all of 16 hp!). He then acquired a brand-new Austin A40 Somerset saloon (TPG 548) in a rather vile eau-de-nil pale green colour. These cars became well-known for their propensity to induce car-sickness due to the type of suspension system they employed, and apocryphally this is the reason why they also had wipe-clean leather upholstery! My official lessons with a driving school were in an older A40 Devon.

After I passed my driving test I was occasionally able to borrow this family car, generally for trips to aerodromes with my girl-friend at the time, a delightful Anglo-Indian girl called Elaine Rogers. I had met Elaine at Guildford Technical College and we had struck up a good friendship; she lived with her parents round the back of Farnborough aerodrome, which was extremely convenient on various occasions!

I also attended my first King's Cup meeting at Baginton (Coventry) the next July in the A40, and was also allowed to borrow it for a two-day trip in August, the first of what turned out to be a series of forays into the South West to see not just aeroplanes, but the country as well. I found it very useful to have various fixed points (aerodromes) in the schedule, around which I built the rest of the trip – I do just the same today! I was able to cover Blackbushe, Andover, Boscombe Down, Thruxton, Yeovilton, Yeovil, Henstridge, Old Sarum, Middle Wallop and Eastleigh.

Mike Jones and I used to visit a lot of aerodromes together. At that time Mike didn't have a car of his own either, but was able to borrow his parents' Morris Minor 1000; he was a fastish driver, although very safe, and I recall the speedometer touching (and staying on) 70 mph on a number of occasions!

Then in 1957 I acquired my first car, a 1937 Austin Seven Ruby, DPO 779; this was purchased from an Austin dealership, Jacksons of Godalming, with whom my father had dealt for many years, and cost me £120, which on reflection was probably rather too much.

But it was certainly in marvellous condition, and very seldom let me down in any way. I kept it until early 1960 and covered a great many miles in it.

My first holiday trip in the Austin Seven was at the end of August with my friend Chris Drake, who in his spare time was building a Fairthorpe Electron Minor sports car single-handed. We included aerodromes at Andover, Thruxton, Upavon, Filton, Lulsgate, Weston-super-Mare, Yeovil, Hurn, Christchurch, Eastleigh, Hamble and Portsmouth. This trip was completed in three days without incident!

The next month I made a special visit to Stansted with Mike Jones to see all the ex-RAF Prentices that Freddie Laker had had stored there. Amongst them I was very pleased to see one bearing my own personalised registration G-APGC, but like most of the others it was never converted and ended up as scrap. In one day we covered Heathrow, Denham, Radlett, Hatfield, Panshanger, Stansted and Stapleford.

In 1958 I ventured further afield for my holiday, and completed a trip that took in Chilbolton, Andover, Thruxton, Middle Wallop, Boscombe Down, Yeovilton, Weston Zoyland, Chivenor, Plymouth, Exeter, Tarrant Rushton, Hurn, Christchurch, Hamble, Eastleigh and Portsmouth. In five days I had no problems apart from a puncture.

That September I was very fortunate to be offered a trip to the Brussels Exhibition. Elaine was by this time working at the Board of Trade in London; their social club had booked a day trip to Brussels, and would I like to go? We flew from Blackbushe in the Viking G-AIVO and had a marvellous day, which included going up to the top of the Atomium. On the return journey, the weather steadily deteriorated until by the time we got back to Blackbushe it was pouring with rain and blowing a gale. Many of the passengers were being sick but, surprisingly, I didn't seem to be affected. The pilot managed to get us down safely on the third attempt.

After this traumatic experience, it was now late at night and I still had to take Elaine home to Farnborough and then drive cross-country back to Woking – well over twenty miles in the Austin Seven. This under normal weather conditions would have been eventful enough, but coming on top of the unpleasant flight it was a bit much. Then right out in the middle of nowhere the feeble headlights failed to warn me that the road ahead was flooded, and before I knew it the car seemed to have been hit by a tidal wave. Somehow I managed to keep going through all the water (fortunately there were 17-inch diameter wheels on an Austin

Seven) but my diary records that I took time off from College the next day!

The major aviation event for me in 1959 was the Woburn Rally on the 2nd May, even better than W.S. Shackleton's Sales Weekend had been just seven days before. For *aficionados* a list of aircraft seen at Woburn is given in Appendix 12. Incidentally, it is the Garden Party atmosphere which pervades this sort of event which I currently try to recreate each year at our Great Vintage Flying Weekend.

In 1959 (and still in my Austin Seven) I became even more adventurous and this time my seven-day itinerary included Eastleigh, Christchurch, Hurn, Portland, Exeter, Plymouth, Culdrose, St. Just, St. Mawgan, St. Eval, Chivenor, Merryfield, Yeovil, Yeovilton, Weston-super-Mare, Lulsgate, Colerne, Keevil, Upavon, Thruxton, Andover and Middle Wallop! I clocked up about a thousand miles on this trip, and once again had just one puncture, this time outside Totnes. However on this trip I also failed to complete the ascent of Porlock Hill when the petrol pump couldn't cope with the strain. Gingerly I turned round and somehow managed to get down the hill safely, in gear and using what there was of the brakes to slow me down; looking back on it now, I must have been immune to the potential for disaster.

At Chivenor I found the Aerovan OO-ERY (ex-G-AJOG) languishing at the back of a hangar; it had been purchased by Devonair in 1958 (they had also been the former owners until 1952 when they had sold the aircraft in Belgium). Their intentions were to renovate the aircraft and then use it on charter work in the West Country, probably including regular flights to Lundy Island, but because of problems relating to the legal ownership of the aircraft nothing ever came of the plans. Later, on a 1961 visit, I was asked if I would like to buy it (probably every visitor was asked the same thing). I politely declined, and what I think was the last surviving Aerovan in the UK was ignominiously burned on a Guy Fawkes bonfire on the 5th of November 1963.

I still have all the records of the aircraft I saw during these 'odysseys' and readers are welcome to get in touch with me if they would like more details.

The University years from 1956 to 1959 had marked an important period in my life when I felt I had finally grown up. The course had quite rightly demanded hard work for much of the time, but this was balanced by periods of very enjoyable recreation. Although I managed to get a reasonable Chemistry Degree in 1959 (I remember telephoning my father for the results during my holiday from a little village in South Devon called Ipplepen), I decided, for various reasons which seemed sensible at the time, to spend one additional year doing a postgraduate teachers' training course. Out of a number of possible Universities, including Exeter, I decided on Southampton if they would accept me, which they did.

At the beginning of 1960, with all the travelling I was doing to Southampton and back, I decided to sell the Austin Seven on to a friend of mine, Bob Powell, who was a hairdresser in Woking. In March I acquired a second-hand Austin A30 van, which had been converted to a four-seater and had an extra window in each side to improve visibility. Only six weeks later, when returning to Southampton on a Sunday evening for the start of the summer term, there was some emergency on the road ahead outside Alton: everyone pulled up sharply, but I was some way back in the queue, and of course the further back you are the less notice you get to slam on the brakes. I finished up by running into the car in front and damaging the radiator and bonnet of the van, whereupon I had to return ignominiously to Woking by taxi. My first accident, and it was my fault.

I had the van repaired but sold it on during the summer holidays, replacing it with an A35 van; this one also had four seats but did not have the extra rear windows, which meant that no purchase tax was payable on the vehicle. So I saved money but didn't have such good visibility. Incidentally, the maximum legal speed limit *anywhere* for a van at that time was 40 mph. After a year or so, when I was earning the enormous (to me) sum of £750 a year as a teacher at Surbiton Grammar School, I bought a brand-new A35 van. I never had any accidents due to the restricted visibility, but was caught out one evening when exceeding the official 40 mph limit. I was due to open with the Witley Pantomime (providing the music) and was late. I failed to see the police car overhauling me on the Guildford bypass until it pulled me in. Despite my acknowledgement that I was in the wrong and that I had to get to Witley, they kept asking me all sorts of questions, seemingly just to make me even later. But I can't remember if the curtain went up on time; I suspect not. After that I bought a proper car, the A40 Farina mentioned in the previous chapter.

CHAPTER 11
ONE DEGREE OVER
(MID-1959–MID-1960)

In September of 1959 I began my last year of University life before starting to earn myself a proper living. I was based at digs in Southampton until the end of the year, doing the first part of a postgraduate teachers' training course, but I used to travel back to Woking for the weekends.

It goes without saying that I was able to visit Eastleigh Airport frequently during those three months; on the 15th October the Hiller XROE-1 Rotocycle one-man helicopter made its maiden flight. The hangars contained mainly Saunders Roe's helicopters including Skeeters and P.531s, but also the Hampshire Aeroplane Club's aircraft and the Currie Wot G-APWT. Regular visiting aircraft were BEA's DC-3s, Silver City's Mk. 32 Superfreighters and Jersey Airlines' Herons. One fine November afternoon four of us piled into the Austin Seven for a trip out to see Stonehenge; needless to say, I got my way and we returned to Southampton via Boscombe Down!

During this first term of the year, we were each seconded to a local school for a fortnight to get a first taste of the teaching experience; I went to Newlands Primary School. Apart from observing and helping out in the classroom, we were also invited to help with the marking of some Eleven Plus examination papers. Several of the answers were memorable; apparently the 'wise men' who visited Jesus brought him gifts of gold, frankincense and mirth [sic]: yes, I suppose he would have needed a a sense of humour when you think what he put through. And one eleven-year-old, asked to compose a sentence using the two words 'while' and 'through,' came up with the following gem: "She loved him for a while, then she said she was through."

I can also recall on that particular day seeing my first new-model Ford Anglia (the one with the undercut rear window, which was manufactured at Ford's plant in Southampton), and thinking how ugly it looked. I got to know the Anglia a lot more intimately when I worked at the Milk Marketing Board.

Early in 1960 I spent a whole term in 'teaching practice' at Hove Grammar School in Sussex (just along the coast from Shoreham!). This was to be my first introduction to actually teaching classes of teenagers. My decision to come again to this area was influenced partly by my desire to be near Shoreham airport again for a while, and also because the parents of a very good ex-school friend of mine, Peter Keeling, lived at Worthing and were happy to have me stay with the family, as I had done in previous years. Sadly, Peter, who had joined the RAF with a Flying Scholarship and was training at Cranwell, had been killed about a year previously in a Vampire Trainer involved in a mid-air collision. He had been engaged to a lovely girl called Jill and they had stayed with our family over Christmas only a month or so before the accident.

The Librarian at Cranwell has sent me a brief account of the scenario, which I now quote:

We regret to record the death in a flying accident of . . . Flight Cadet Peter David Keeling. . . . Flight Cadet Keeling came from Lancing College with a Flying Scholarship in January 1957. He joined No. 76 Entry. A hockey player for the College, he also took part in athletics and cross-country running for his Squadron.

31-Jan-1959 WR194 Vampire 9 0.5 miles east of RAF Cranwell This aircraft returned to the airfield and joined the dead side of the circuit whilst another aircraft was completing an overshoot. As the other aircraft turned starboard it collided with this aircraft, which was crossing the upwind end of the runway. Both aircraft immediately crashed. The pilot of this aircraft failed to make a call that he was joining the circuit and maintained an inadequate lookout.

Flight Cadet Michael DICKINSON, 21.

31-Jan-1959 XE936 Vampire T.11 0.5 miles east of Cranwell Mid-air collision with WR194 as outlined above.

Flight Lieutenant Donald Gilliland MURCHIE, 28, Pilot Instructor.

Flight Cadet Peter David KEELING, 20, Student pilot.

Peter was a good friend and I still miss him.

At Hove I was put under the wing of one of the science teachers, Roger Clarke, who has remained a good friend over all the intervening years. He taught continuously at the same school (now a Comprehensive) for his entire working life until retiring recently, since when he has been even busier than before.

As part of the year's course I had to write a postgraduate thesis and had decided upon the subject "The Social Development of Adolescents," a bit of a cheek really when you consider that I was only a few years past being one myself. Much of the thesis was already written by this time, but the headmaster at Hove allowed me to prepare a questionnaire which was distributed amongst the pupils for them to fill in in their spare time. (Some were happier than others to oblige – I had several questionnaires returned with additional comments such as "Do you think, or, like some people, do you not?")

The results were to be interpreted by myself, using statistical analysis, to define a "Sociability Index" for boys of all ages between twelve and eighteen, i.e. an indication of how successfully they were interacting with other people as they grew up. The results showed that, statistically, it wasn't until the age of about seventeen that boys began to mature socially in any noticeable manner. But perhaps this was not so surprising, on reflection. I would have liked to repeat the study with a girls' school: a hunch tells me that the results would have been quite different.

I had quite a pleasant surprise early in 1960. I often used to go out to the cinema or the local theatre in the evenings, and one week I noticed that the local repertory company were going to be putting on a play with two guest stars; one was Brook Williams, with whom you may remember I had been a pupil at Cottesmore school some ten years before, and the other was a film star called Jackie Lane, my opinion of whom at that time was that she was the most beautiful girl that had ever existed! I duly went to see the play, which turned out to be more amusing than was intended, largely because an actor doing a scene with Jackie forgot his lines, and there was then much discussion between them about the gestation period of a ferret [sic] until they eventually found their way back to the script.

Afterwards I went backstage, and Brook Williams, who appeared genuinely pleased to see me, suggested that we go and have a drink at the local pub along with the other star of the play, Jackie Lane herself! It was a strange feeling actually to come face-to-face with someone I had idolised in my youthful innocence, but in fact she was not only a very pretty girl indeed, she had real acting ability and at the same time remained natural and so was very easy to get on with. I often wonder what happened to her in the longer term; I do know that her elder sister, Mara, who attracted a lot more publicity, finished up married to an Italian Count.

During the Easter break, two events I attended stand out, one as being – frankly – incredibly boring to onlookers, although I thought I ought to witness it at least once: this was the annual World Marbles Championship played outside a pub at Tinsley Green, near Gatwick. The second was to me infinitely more absorbing, and was the first motor racing meeting at Goodwood Circuit where aircraft were also encouraged to attend. In this and subsequent years, this meeting proved to be one of the first events in the calendar of events not to be missed. Details of the aircraft present are given in Appendix 13.

For the summer (and final) term, I had been recommended to a different landlady as my previous digs were not available. However this time I was in a part of Southampton near the railway yards, where every night without fail I was subjected to the ancient Chinese torture of 'shun ting' and was frequently woken up by the clanging of freight-wagon buffers and the frantic puffing of steam locos as they tried to get a grip on the wet rails. I must say that I have never slept really soundly ever since that time. My landlady had recently been divorced, which was the reason for her taking in lodgers, but her desire to mother me became too overpowering, and I didn't stay there any longer than I needed to.

There was a lot of preparation to be done prior to the final examinations, which we were free to do whenever and wherever we wished. When at home studying, I had found it refreshing to stop every now and then to get up and look at an aeroplane as it passed overhead; it kept me from getting too bogged down mentally. Now I wondered if I could put a similar technique into operation; where could I go that was quiet, yet offered a good view of all the comings and goings at Eastleigh? After a bit of research, I came up with the perfect answer – the local cemetery! After all, nowhere could be quieter than that and, what was more, it was situated right at the western end of the runway. So I used to drive out there and park for a couple of hours in the afternoon whilst I revised for my exams. Many of the movements were still the BEA DC-3s on the Channel Islands run and the Superfreighters of Silver City. Saunders Roe did the test-flying of their helicopters from here, and apart from the prototype Wasps there were plenty of Skeeters around, along with the first two Currie Wots and the other aircraft of the Hampshire Aeroplane Club.

The time approached for the exams and I did not want to go back to the digs by the shunting yards – sleep was too precious. I booked myself in to a local guest house, which was more expensive but which enabled me to have the freedom to come and go as I needed. This worked well, and happily I passed these exams too.

After my finals were over, I took on a holiday job just down the road from home, at the local Mercedes dealers. I was part-time car valeter, washer and polisher, and occasionally filled up cars with petrol. On one occasion, a few minutes after a gleaming black Merc had pulled away after a top-up with oil, it returned; the driver definitely had an irate look on his face, and when he wound down his window, he told me that he had been driving along and the bonnet had suddenly sprung up, cutting off all forward vision. My fault – I hadn't secured the catch properly; that could have been nasty. I was also occasionally detailed to deliver repaired or serviced cars to their owners, so had the opportunity to drive some vehicles very different from my A35 van. I was a bit cheeky one day and turned up outside my girl friend's house in West Byfleet in a sumptious new black convertible. All the kids in the street closed in on me to have a good look, and I think that Rosemary, who of course also came out to see who on earth it could be, was rather embarrassed by the whole thing!

I finally managed to get as far as Southend that August to see the remainder of Freddie Laker's Prentices that were not at Stansted. It was a long haul from Woking and back in a day, especially as I was running in a new van.

The year (and the decade) was rounded off in what I thought was an extremely appropriate manner; my former schoolfriend, Tim Foster, who had emigrated to Canada in 1956, paid a brief visit home over Christmas 1960, and took both David Timmis and myself flying from Biggin Hill on Boxing Day in Auster 5 G-APBE (this aircraft had been offered as a prize by the *"Daily Mirror"* a few years previously).

When I had finally completed my formal education that summer I had decided that I would take up teaching science, although I don't think I had ever considered myself dedicated enough to the profession to make it a lifetime career. Probably the reality was that I didn't really know what I wanted to do with my life. But things were very different in those days when you came out of College with a degree – there was no problem in getting a job. I did get one, and taught science subjects for a couple of years at Surbiton Grammar School, but began to feel that any teacher worth his salt should know something about the commercial side of life. After attending a local industries exhibition one afternoon I was offered a job at Gala Cosmetics at Surbiton as their first research chemist (where I met Honor, my wife-to-be). It didn't take me long to realise that I was not cut out to be a teacher all my life. After two years there I finished up the sixties at the Milk Marketing Board, when I had opportunities to travel all over the UK and abroad.

In 1970, after a brief spell at Williams of Hounslow (who made colourings for food and cosmetics), when it took me over an hour to commute 15 miles, and all work came to a full stop every couple of minutes or so as a jet took off from Heathrow, I decided I'd had enough of the London area. I managed to get a job in Shaftesbury with a frozen food company, Dorset Foods, and all three of us (by then we had a young son, James) moved to Dorset lock, stock and barrel. We have been here ever since, and have had several businesses of our own, but that's another story.

Looking back now, I am convinced that the most fascinating and formative period of my life really ended in 1960 when I was qualified professionally and needed to take on the serious responsibilities of life for the first time. I also moved away from home that July into a bedsitter. So everything seemed to coincide within a few months: I got my degree, I moved house, I got my first proper job.

On the aviation front the American invasion was getting under way. Would this affect my perennial interest? Well, I must confess that the newly-available Pipers and Cessnas did not, for me, have the same appeal as the more traditional British-built machines. In September 1959, Vigors Aviation had held a sales weekend at Fair Oaks, "Piperama," where they displayed new aircraft such as the Super Cub, Comanche, Tripacer and Apache. This heralded the beginning of the 'out with the old, in with the new' period following the relaxation of import restrictions, which was of course inevitable eventually. To begin with, American aircraft were imported via Eire and so carried Irish registrations. Later, many were flown into Heathrow in crates and reassembled at Kidlington, or occasionally even flown directly out of Heathrow.

The demise of many British-made aircraft continued into the early sixties, especially of the wooden ones, which were becoming increasingly expensive to maintain and were also suspected of suffering from glue failure. For this reason most Miles and Percival aircraft were eventually broken up, although Austers and many de Havilland types were not affected as they were of metal construction. With hindsight it now seems as if a lot of this wholesale destruction may been completely unnecessary. As far as Miles aircraft were concerned, the glue-quality problem which led to eventual failure in one or two instances is thought to have originated during a short period of time in the beginning of 1947, when the winter weather was so extreme that the factory heating at Woodley was unable to cope adequately with what was expected of it (and, of course, fuel supplies were then very restricted anyway). But by the time the facts became known, it was too late. I have a copy of a report from Cranfield, kindly given to me by Michael Jones of the Tiger Club, in which the results of glue tests carried out on Geminis and Proctors did not seem really to justify wholesale breaking-up.

In the late fifties and early sixties there were also other changes of a more unsettling nature that began to force themselves on our consciousness. Despite the predictions that had been given in a lecture that I had attended back in 1955 on the possibilities for interplanetary travel, which were that space flight would be an impossibility for at least twenty years due to the lack of both a suitable fuel and also materials for building a space vehicle, the Russians (who apparently were not aware of these restrictions) had successfully launched Sputnik on the 4th October 1957, and now the world was looking very much smaller and definitely more unstable.

Can you remember what you were doing when the Cuba missile crisis broke in 1962? I can, only too well, and I remember being resigned to the possibility that everything we had been working for could well come to an abrupt end. Fortunately common sense prevailed. I am reminded of a spoof commercial for paint devised by Spike Milligan which, against a backdrop of a horrendous atom bomb explosion with the huge black mushroom cloud, recommended: "For a really professional finish, use 'Nuclear.'"

But as I look back now, I am deeply appreciative of all the opportunities that were available for ordinary youngsters like myself during the fifties, although we had to use plenty of initiative if we were to make the most of them.

Since I first had the idea nearly ten years ago that I would like to record my experiences in writing, and subsequently published the first (and rather amateur) edition of *"The Fifties Revisited,"* I have become more involved with aviation matters than ever before and have got to know a great many really dedicated people in the business, some of whom were my boyhood 'idols.' What better way could there be for a lifetime aircraft enthusiast to bring his working days to a close than to publish books about the period of aviation history in which he was personally involved in a small way?

But how I wish that the world today was as straightforward to understand, and as safe to live in as it seemed to be when I was growing up. I do not think I envy today's parents, nor indeed their children.

APPENDIX 1
EAST ANGLIAN FLYING SERVICES (LATER CHANNEL AIRWAYS) AT SHOREHAM

During the early fifties, scheduled passenger services were flown via Shoreham by East Anglian Flying Services. The main operating base was Southend, and services flew either to Ipswich, or via Rochester to Shoreham, and thence to Portsmouth, Jersey, Guernsey and, later, Paris (Le Bourget) and Belgium. In 1952 the aircraft operated were Dragon Rapides G-AKJZ, G-AKRN and G-AKSC, and these were joined in 1953 by G-AEMH. In 1954-55 the J/1 Autocrat G-AGXP, Auster 5 G-ANHZ and Proctor 4 G-ANGM acted as 'back-up' aircraft, and in 1955 the fleet was further enlarged to include three Dove 1 aircraft; G-ANVU first visited Shoreham on the 7th May, G-AOBZ on the 1st June, and G-AOCE on the 2nd July. The service operated throughout a wide range of weather conditions, and the only reported mishaps during this period occurred when Dragon Rapide G-AKSC force-landed on a beach in Jersey on the 25th July 1954, and Dove G-ANVU suffered a tyre-burst on landing at Shoreham on the 15th July 1955.

The airline was honoured to have on its staff the first fully-qualified female airline pilot in the UK, Jackie Moggridge, and other Captains were Dan Burgess and Messrs Murray, Parsons, Pascoe, Taylor, Whellem and Willmot. Even the founder of the airline, Jack Jones, did the occasional stint.

In the early fifties the standard colour scheme for all the Company's aircraft was as follows: silver wings with large registration in red covering both wings, white upper fuselage, silver lower fuselage, with red cheat line and registration. When the Doves entered service in 1955, they sported green trim instead of red, and carried smaller registrations under one wing and on the fin, as was by then becoming current practice. The two Rapides still with the airline (G-AEMH and G-AKRN) were also resprayed in these colours.

The fleet was enlarged further in 1957 with Dove G-AOZW, and my records show that towards the end of the decade the airline, now operating as Channel Airways (although still officially registered as EAFS), had used in the past, or were still operating, a fleet comprising the following aircraft:

G-AEMH	Dragon Rapide	G-ANGM	Proctor 4
G-AGXP	Auster J/I Autocrat	G-ANGN	Proctor 4
G-AHOU	Viking 1B		(not converted)
G-AHOZ	Viking 1B	G-ANGO	Proctor 4
G-AHPH	Viking 1B		(not converted)
G-AHRB	Dove 1	G-ANGP	Proctor 4
G-AICT	Bristol Freighter Mk. 21 (Wayfarer)	G-ANHZ	(not converted) Auster 5
G-AIFO	Bristol Freighter Mk. 21 (Wayfarer)	G-ANKG	Tiger Moth
		G-ANVU	Dove 1
G-AKJZ	Dragon Rapide	G-AOBZ	Dove 1
G-AKRN	Dragon Rapide	G-AOCE	Dove 1
G-AKSC	Dragon Rapide	G-AOZW	Dove 1
G-AMDZ	DC-3	G-APAG	Dove 1

APPENDIX 2
TYPICAL CLUB-OWNED AIRCRAFT
SEEN AT SHOREHAM DURING 1952-1955

During the early fifties a number of Flying Clubs and Schools used Shoreham as a cross-country destination, and so their aircraft were seen fairly often. For the record, here is a list of these operators, together with details of typical aircraft and with their colour schemes as I remember them (I cannot guarantee full accuracy!).

AEROCONTACTS
Base: Gatwick.
Typical aircraft: G-AMJN Tiger Moth.
Colour Scheme: Red fuselage and silver wings.

AIR SERVICE TRAINING
Base: Hamble.
Typical aircraft: G-AMSV, G-AMSW, G-AMSX DC-3, G-AIAT, G-AIAX, G-ALTP, G-ALTR Oxford, G-AMUC, G-AMUD, G-AMUE, G-AMUF, G-AMUG, G-AMUH Chipmunk, G-AMUI, G-AMUJ J/5F Aiglet Tr., G-AKXP, G-AKXR Auster 5.
Colour scheme: Black fuselage with silver registration, and silver wings with black registration. Although most of these aircraft overflew Shoreham regularly, they never landed there until 1957 (G-AKXP was the first to do so on the 17th June).

AIRWAYS AERO ASSOCIATIONS
Base: Denham, later Croydon.
Typical aircraft: G-AMTA, G-AMTB, G-AMTC, G-AMTD, G-AMTE J/5F Aiglet Tr., G-ANDE, G-ANEW Tiger Moth.
Colour scheme: Silver overall with blue trim and registration.

BRITISH AIR TRANSPORT/REDHILL FLYING CLUB
Base: Redhill.
Typical aircraft: G-AJRT, G-AKJV, G-ALFE Hawk Tr. 3, G-AGVJ, G-AHCK, G-AJEH J/1 Autocrat.
Colour scheme: Silver overall with blue trim, registration, and stripe down the rear of the rudder.

CHRISTCHURCH AERO CLUB
Base: Christchurch.
Typical aircraft: G-AKGR Hawk Tr. 3, G-ADWO, G-AHVY, G-AKZZ Tiger Moth, G-AHUM Taylorcraft Plus D (sold in 1954 to D.G.S. Cotter at Gatwick), G-AFWN, G-AHAT J/1 Autocrat.
Colour scheme: Initially, G-AHUM, G-ADWO and G-AKZZ were finished in a very distinctive colour scheme comprising olive green fuselage with silver registration, and silver wings. G-AHVY was all-silver with yellow trim. The Autocrats were in silver with red trim. Later, Club Tiger Moths were painted in an all-yellow scheme.

CROYDON FLYING CLUB
Base: Croydon.
Typical aircraft: G-AHHX Taylorcraft Plus D.
Colour scheme: Silver overall with black registration.

EXPERIMENTAL FLYING GROUP
Base: Croydon.
Typical aircraft: G-AITN, G-ALIO, G-AMBM Hawk Tr. 3.
Colour scheme: Finished in eau-de-nil (pale blue-green) with dark blue registration.

FORD RNVR FLYING GROUP
Base: RNAS Ford.
Typical aircraft: G-ANCS, G-AOBX (T7187) Tiger Moth.
Colour scheme: The former was silver overall, the latter was kept in service colours i.e. silver with yellow training bands and black serial.

HAMPSHIRE AEROPLANE CLUB
Base: Eastleigh.
Typical aircraft: G-ALUA Zaunköenig (grey with black & white chequerboard rudder), G-ADKC Hornet Moth (dark blue), G-AHHW J/1 Autocrat, G-AHZH Tiger Moth (both silver with red trim). Later in the fifties the Club colours comprised a red fuselage with cream top-decking, e.g. the DH.86B G-ACZP wore this scheme.

HOOKWOOD FLYING GROUP
Base: Gatwick.
Typical aircraft: G-AFWM Taylorcraft Plus C-2, G-AHAD Taylorcraft Plus D, G-AOEH (ex-N79854) Aeronca Champion.
Colour scheme: Silver overall with black registration (but the Champion may have had a white upper fuselage).

LONDON AERO CLUB
Base: Panshanger.
Typical aircraft: G-ADUR Hornet Moth, G-AGYN J/1 Autocrat, G-AFOJ Moth Minor, G-AKDN Chipmunk.
Colour scheme: Silver overall with yellow trim and registration.

NIGHTSCALE FLYING SERVICES/DENHAM FLYING CLUB
Base: Denham.
Typical aircraft: G-AHAI, G-AHUG, G-AIIU Taylorcraft Plus D.
Colour scheme: Silver overall with dark blue registration.

PENGUIN FLYING CLUB
Base: Gatwick.
Typical aircraft: G-AHGW, G-AHHB, G-AHKO Taylorcraft Plus D.
Colour scheme: Silver overall with black registration.

ROYAL ARTILLERY AERO CLUB
Base: Thruxton.
Typical aircraft: G-AGYI, G-AJAE J/1 Autocrat.
Colour scheme: Grey with red trim, cowling and registration.

ROYAL NAVAL FLYING CLUB
Base: Lee-on-Solent.
Typical aircraft: G-AISA, G-AISB Tipsy B Srs. 1.
Colour scheme: Red overall with white trim and registration.

SHORT BROS. & HARLAND FLYING CLUB
Base: Rochester.
Typical aircraft: G-ALIM Hawk Tr. 3, G-AMIU, G-AMIV Tiger Moth.
Colour scheme: Silver overall with black registration.

SOUTHERN AERO CLUB
Base: Shoreham.
Typical aircraft: Hawk Trainers G-AITS (silver with red trim and registration) and G-AIZK (grey with red trim and registration). G-AITS crashed on the 16th August 1955, but G-AIZK remained with the Club until long after its C. of A. expired in November 1956, until sometime in 1959 at least, after which it finished its days in Norfolk. Until sometime in 1953 the Club also operated Taylorcraft Plus D G-AHVR (red overall with white trim and registration, ex-Midland Aero Club). It seems as though the SAC were in the habit of purchasing their aircraft from the Midland Flying Club at Elmdon as, apart from G-AHVR, they acquired two Tiger Moths from that source in 1955 viz. G-AKXO and G-ALVP; these both appeared initially in the red overall scheme but this was later changed to silver with red trim and registration. In 1956 G-AOIS was purchased from Thruxton to enlarge the fleet.

SOUTHEND AERO CLUB (MUNICIPALLY-OWNED)
Base: Southend.
Typical aircraft: G-AIZY, G-AJEO, G-AJUE J/1 Autocrat, G-AMFP J/5B Autocar.

Colour scheme: Silver overall with red trim and registration.
SOUTHERN FLYING SCHOOLS
Base: Portsmouth.
Typical aircraft: G-AHHP, G-AJAB, G-AJIS J/1 Autocrat, G-AMHF, G-AMHG Tiger Moth.
Colour scheme: Silver overall with red trim and registration. G-AJIS flew for a while during the summer of 1954 with a patch under the port wing which caused me to record it initially as G-AIIS.
SURREY AVIATION
Base: Croydon.
Typical aircraft: G-ANRY, G-ANSG, G-ANYN, G-AOBO Tiger Moth, G-AELO Hornet Moth.
Colour scheme: Mid-blue overall with yellow tail assembly, trim and registration.
UNIVERSAL FLYING SERVICES
Base: Fair Oaks.
Typical aircraft: G-AHRM, G-AHRN, G-AHUT, G-AJOA, G-ANDF, G-ANDG, G-ANDH, G-ANOM, G-ANOZ, G-ANPB, G-ANUD, G-AOAC, G-AODS, G-AODU Tiger Moth, G-ALUX, G-AMBN Hawk Tr. 3, G-AHSO, G-AIGU, G-AJDV J/1 Autocrat.
Colour scheme: Finished in silver overall with green registration. Later the Austers acquired a green cheat line also. G-AIGU was purchased by the Club early in 1955 and was the first of the two later converted by them to J/1N Alpha standard. G-AHSO was sold to the Bristol & Wessex Aero Club in 1956.

The Hawk Tr. 3 G-ALUX was sold to a private owner (a builder from Wimbledon, Mr William Way) in 1953, and was then repainted with a black fuselage and pale cream wings, cheat line and registration; a large dice was featured on the cowling. Sometime at the end of the fifties it was sold to Henry Pelham, the owner of Thruxton aerodrome and circuit.

UFS aircraft were individually numbered in 1956 by painting a digit on each side of the cowling in black as follows:
G-AHSO: 1, G-AJDV: 2, G-AIGU: 3, G-AHRM: 4, G-ANDG: 5, G-ANUD: 6, G-ANPB: 7, G-ANOZ: 8, G-AODU: 9, G-ANOM: no number, but a skull and crossbones motif, G-AODS: 11.

By mid-1957 G-ANOM had inherited '1' (G-AHSO had been sold), G-AOAC carried '8,' G-AODS carried '10,' and the two Chipmunks acquired by the Club carried '11' (G-AORL, named 'Diamond Lil') and '12' (G-AORK, named 'Klondyke Kate').
WILTSHIRE SCHOOL OF FLYING
Base: Thruxton.
Typical aircraft: G-AKZN Proctor 3, G-AGVP, G-AIGC, G-AIZW J/1 Autocrat, G-ACEZ, G-ALSH, G-AMBI, G-AMHP Tiger Moth.
Colour scheme: Finished in silver overall with red registration, trim and cowling panels.

Other frequent visitors to Shoreham on business were the Dragon Rapides of (a) Marshall's Flying Services of Cambridge (e.g. G-AGZO, G-AHED, G-AHLM, G-AKNN), painted silver overall with large green registration, (b) Don Everall Aviation of Elmdon (e.g. G-AGDM, G-AGLR), silver overall with yellow registration. They were carrying jockeys, trainers etc. to the race meetings at Brighton. Also a regular visitor for the same purpose was 'Flightways' Gemini G-AKFY.

The two aircraft of Longford Engineering Co. Ltd. (LEC Refrigeration) used to pay the occasional visit from the Company airfield at nearby Bognor Regis: they were G-AJVC Messenger 2A and G-AJYY J/5B Autocar; they were both replaced later by G-ALMU Gemini 3A.

APPENDIX 3
AIRCRAFT AT SHOREHAM ON THE 22ND JUNE 1952 (MY FIRST DAY OF 'SPOTTING')

A Lunch Patrol was planned, but was cancelled because of a low cloud base. However the weather cleared during the afternoon.

Resident Aircraft
Hawk Tr. 3:   G-AITS, G-AIZK
Aries: G-AMDJ
Aerovan 6:   G-AKHF
Proctor 4:   G-AJMH
Proctor 5:   G-AHBI
Taylorcraft Plus D: G-AHVR
Swallow 2:   G-AFHS
Chilton: G-AFSV

Visiting Aircraft
Autocrat J/1:   G-AGXU, G-AHAU, G-AIPZ, G-AJUP
Autocar J/5B: G-AJYO, G-AMFO
Hawk Tr. 3:   G-AFBS, G-AKRV, G-ALFE
Taylorcraft Plus D: G-AHKO, G-AHSB
Auster 4:   G-ALYD
Auster 5:   G-AIKC
Proctor 1:   G-AHVA, G-AILP
Proctor 3:   G-AIKJ
Proctor 5:   G-AHGJ
Messenger 2A: G-AIEK, G-AILL
Messenger 4:   G-AKKG
Messenger 4A: G-ALBE
Gemini 1A: G-AJWF, G-AKHJ
Ercoupe: G-AKFC
Whitney Straight: G-AEUJ
Chipmunk: WK631, WK634
Anson 12:   PH662
Meteor 8:   WF753 Meteor 8 (overflight)

APPENDIX 4
LINCOLNS SEEN OVER SHOREHAM, MAY 1953

RA658	RE320	RE417	SX975
RA661	RE322	RE423	SX976
RA662	RE323	RF335	SX978
RA672	RE345	RF336	SX979
RA673	RE347	RF346	SX982
RA677	RE348	RF349	SX983
RA681	RE360	RF446	SX984
RA684	RE361	RF460	SX985
RA685	RE368	RF555	SX986
RE289	RE372	RF565	SX987
RE295	RE397	RF575	SX988
RE300	RE400	SX933	SX989
RE301	RE407	SX937	WD125
RE304	RE415	SX944	WD148

APPENDIX 5
AIRCRAFT SEEN AT RNAS FORD (1953-1955)

PRIVATE VISIT, MARCH 1953

Anson T.21:	WB465
Attacker:	WA521, WK324
Dominie:	NF881
Firefly 1:	Z1901
Firefly 5:	VT429, VT473
Firefly 6:	WD849, WD857, WJ104
Harvard:	FX214, KF289
Meteor T.7:	VW443, WS103
Sea Fury T.20:	VX608
Vampire 5:	VZ148
Sea Fury FB.11:	WH617
Sea Hawk:	WF162, WF163, WF166, WF167, WF173, WF174, WM902, WM904, WM905
Sea Vampire:	VV152
Sea Venom:	WK379, WM500, WM501
Wyvern:	VZ766

ATC CADETS' VISIT, JUNE 13TH 1953

Anson:	MH117
Attacker:	WZ282
Avenger:	XB364, XB444
Dragon Rapide:	G-AMJK
Firebrand:	EK627, EK773
Firefly 1:	Z1901
Firefly 4:	DK508, DK528, DK550, MB721, PP605, TW722, TW723, VG962, VG965, VG974, VG993, VH132
Firefly 5:	VT394
Firefly 6:	WD845, WD849, WD862, WD889
Gannet:	WN347, WN348
Meteor T.7:	WS103
Meteor F.8:	WK784
Sea Fury FB.11:	VW583, VW584, VW649, VX668, VX690, WE786, WF617, WG593, WG661, WH231, WH594, WH617
Sea Fury T.20:	VX300, VX309
Sea Vampire:	VV138, VV149, VV150
Vampire T.11:	XA111
Wyvern:	VZ752, VZ758, VZ759, VZ761, VZ773, VZ785

AIR DAY, JULY 25TH 1953

Attacker:	WK320, WK321, WK323, WK325, WK328, WK331, WK332, WK336, WK338, WK340, WK341, WK342, WP275, WP279, WP286, WP288, WP292, WP294, WP296, WP297, WP298, WP304
Expeditor:	FT994, KP110
Firebrand:	EK664
Firefly 4:	MB721, TW723, VG965, VG966
Firefly 5:	VT426, VX413, VX425
Firefly 6:	WD916, WD918, WD920, WD922, WH628
Firefly 8:	WJ104, WJ118
Harvard:	EZ372, KF537
Hawk Tr. 3:	G-AITN

Hiller 360:	XB481
Meteor T.7:	WA600, WL335, WS903
Sea Fury FB.11:	VX608
Sea Fury T.20:	VX300
Skyraider:	WT946
Sea Hornet:	VW954
Sea Vampire:	VG701, VV139, VV148
Sea Hawk:	WF168, WM905
Sea Prince:	WF137, WP311
Tiger Moth:	NL879
W/S S.51 Dragonfly:	WG708, WN496, WP495
W/S S.55 Whirlwind:	WW339

AIR DAY, JULY 3RD 1954

Attacker:	WP298
Avenger:	XB310, XB314, XB358, XB359, XB365, XB368
Chipmunk:	WP976
Firefly 4:	DK449, MB530, MB723, PP478, VH127
Firefly 5:	VT429
Firefly 6:	WD849, WD908, WD922
Firefly 8:	WJ104, WJ115, WJ119
Glider (unknown make, ex-German):	VS201
Harvard:	KF526, KF537
Meteor T.7:	WH219, WS103
Proctor 4:	G-ANGM
Sea Balliol:	WL719
Sea Fury FB.11:	TF969, VR926, VX620, WE693, WE785, WF617, WG593, WG601, WH594, WH612, WJ321
Sea Fury T.20:	VZ368, VZ369
Sea Hawk:	WF179, WF182, WF184, WF190, WF194, WF203, WF206, WF207, WF208, WF209, WF211, WF212, WF213, WF244, WF252, WF253, WF263, WF264, WF266, WF267, WF274
Sea Venom:	WM515
Swordfish:	NF389
Skyraider:	WT950
Tiger Moth:	NL879
Vampire T.11:	XA130
W/S S.51 Dragonfly:	WG720, WN496, WP495
Wyvern:	VZ778, VZ779, VZ780, VZ781, VZ782, VZ793, VZ797, WL876, WL879

ATC CADETS' VISIT, MARCH 24TH 1955

Firefly 5:	VT363, WB428, WD851
Firefly 8:	WJ196
Gannet:	WN453
Meteor NF.11:	WM154
Seafire:	SX368
Sea Balliol:	WL719, WL720
Sea Fury T.20:	VZ349, WZ655
Sea Hawk:	WM905, WM906, WM916
Sea Prince:	WP311, WV133
Sea Vampire:	VV136, VV150
Sea Venom:	WM547, WM554
Skyraider:	WT761, WT966
Tiger Moth:	T7187, G-ANCS

Vampire T.11:   XA110, XG747, XG768
Wyvern: VZ784, VZ785, VZ787, VZ789, VZ790, VZ791, VZ794, WL879, WL883
W/S S.51 Dragonfly: WN496, WP495

APPENDIX 6
AIRCRAFT ATTENDING THE PASSING OUT PARADE AT CRANWELL, 28TH JULY 1953

N.B. Serial numbers *not* followed by an asterisk are the only ones known for certain.

J/1 Autocrat   G-AJIE
Chipmunk: WD373, WG353, WK516, WK518, WK563, WK565, WG566, WK556, WK557, WK559, WK560, WK561, WK562, WK567, WK568, WK569, WK570, WK581, WK586, WP844, WP845, WP853, WP854, WP855, WP859, WP860, WP862, WP866, WP869, WP903, WZ865, WZ874 (all believed part of the College fleet except for the first two listed)
Anson: PH698*, TX154, TX173*, TX256*, VM308*, VM315*, VM317*, VM330*, VM361*, VM378*, VM408*, VV257, VV258*, VV294*, VV325*
Canberra: WH650*
Dakota: KN446*, KP208*
Devon: VP958*, VP961 (the Duke of Edinburgh's aircraft), VP963*, VP966*, VP968*, VP974*, VP975*, WB534*
Harvard: ET 271*, FS752 (coded AH), FT354, KF703
Meteor 4:   RA368 + 7 more unidentified
Nighthawk: G-AGWT
Oxford: LB410*
Proctor 4:   NP178*
Shackleton 2:   VP287*, WB822*, WL751*
Spitfire: EP770*
Valetta: VL282*, VX576, VW820*, WD168*
Varsity: WF419*

112

APPENDIX 7
AIRCRAFT SEEN AT GATWICK, 17TH NOVEMBER 1953

Attacker:	WA520
Autocar J/5B:	G-AMNB
Bell 47:	G-AKFA, G-AKFB
Bristol 171 Sycamore:	G-ALSR, G-AMWG, G-AMWH
Bristol Freighter 21:	9698 (RCAF)
Consul:	TJ-ABB, TJ-ABE
Dragon Rapide:	G-AKPA, G-AKSD
Hornet Moth:	G-AMZO
Marathon 1:	G-AMEO
Moth Minor:	G-AFNI
Proctor 5:	G-AIET
Seafire:	SR463, SR513, SR542, SR640, SW786, SW792, SW850, SW868, SW912, SW917
Sea Hornet:	VR850, VZ680
Tiger Moth:	G-ANBY, G-ANCK, G-ANCL

APPENDIX 8
AIRCRAFT AT SHOREHAM DURING THE VISIT OF THE HUREL-DUBOIS HD-31, 25TH–28TH MARCH 1954

Aiglet Tr. J/5F:	G-AMTA, G-AMTC, G-AMUJ (overflight)
Anson 21:	WJ514
Auster AOP.6:	VX120
Autocrat J/1:	G-AFWN, G-AGTY, G-AHSO, G-AIGE
DC-3:	G-AMSV (overflight)
Chipmunk:	G-AMUC (overflight), G-AMUG (overflight), WK548, WK581, WP763, WZ853, WZ877
Devon:	HW519 (overflight – Indian A/F)
Expeditor:	33944 (overflight – US Navy)
Gannet:	WN350 (overflight)
Harvard:	KH384
Hawk Tr. 3:	G-AJRT
Hurel Dubois HD-31:	F-WFKU
Meteor NF.14:	WZ240 (overflight)
Moth Minor:	G-AFPD
Oxford:	N4783
Percival Q.6:	G-AEYE
Proctor 1:	G-AHFY, G-AHGA, G-AILP
Taylorcraft Plus D:	G-AHHB, G-AHKO, G-AIXB
Whitney Straight:	G-AEVG

APPENDIX 9
AIRCRAFT SEEN AT RAE FARNBOROUGH, AIR CADETS' VISIT, 18TH MARCH 1955

Anson 19:	VP509
Apollo:	VX224
Ashton:	WB494
Attacker:	WA527, WA529
Auster 3:	G-AHLK
Avenger:	KE416, XB296, XB308
Brigand:	RF237
Bristol 171 Sycamore:	VW904
Canberra B.2:	WD947, WH661, WH776, WJ635, WJ842
Canberra PR.3:	WE146
Canberra T.4:	WJ867
Chipmunk:	WB549, WD385
Comet 1:	G-ALYS, G-ALYU, G-ANAV
Devon:	VP959, VP979, XA879
Firefly 5:	VX428
Gannet:	VR546
Hastings:	WD480
Hunter F.1:	WT564
Lancaster:	RT690
Lincoln:	RF528, SX971, WD125, WD129
Marathon 1:	G-AMHV
Meteor F.4:	EE403, EE519, EE522, RA424
Meteor T.7:	WA639, WA690, WB134, WL337, WL447, WL377, WL478
Meteor F.8:	VZ460, WH231
Meteor PR.9:	WX979
Pembroke:	WV710
Proctor 1:	G-AHAB
Provost:	WV551
Sea Hawk:	WF147, WV828
Sea Hornet:	VL621
Shackleton 1:	VP285
Short SA.4:	VX161
Spitfire 14:	G-ALGT
Storch:	VP546, VX154
Swift:	WK199
Tiger Moth:	G-AMCM
Valetta 1:	VW197, VW217, VW218, VX541
Valetta 3:	WJ463
Valiant:	WP201, WP202
Vampire F.3:	VT805
Vampire FB.5:	WG801
Vampire T.11:	WZ419
Venom:	WE501
Varsity:	WF381, WJ937, WL679

APPENDIX 10
AIRCRAFT SEEN AT CROYDON, 10TH MARCH 1956

Autocrat:	G-AHHS
Aiglet Tr.:	G-AMTA, G-AMTC
Auster 5:	G-ANIK, G-ANKI
Bell 47:	G-AODI
Bonanza:	G-AOAM
Consul:	G-AIAH, G-AIKT, G-AIOW, G-AJNE, G-ALTZ
DC-3:	G-AMPZ, G-AMSV, G-AMYW*, G-AMZG, G-ANEG, G-ANTB, G-ANTC
Dingbat:	G-AFJA (in pieces)
Dragon Rapide:	G-AFFB, G-AGUF, G-AGWP, G-AKNY, G-AKZP
Dove 2:	G-AMHM
Falcon:	G-ADFH (broken up)
GAL.42 Cygnet:	G-AGAX
Gemini 1A:	G-AKEG, G-AKEI, G-AKHC
Gemini 3A:	G-AMKZ, G-AMME
Gipsy Moth:	G-ABJJ
Hawk Major:	G-ADWT
Hawk Tr. 3:	G-AJGM (wings only), G-AKPL (wings only), G-ALIO
Heron 1:	G-ANLN
Heron 2:	G-ANUO
Leopard Moth:	G-ACLL, G-AIYS
Messenger 2A:	G-AILL, G-AKKO
Messenger 4A:	G-AKVZ (fuselage only)
Mosquito:	CF-IMB
Oxford:	NM776
Percival Q.6:	G-AEYE
Prince 1:	G-ALWH
Proctor 3:	G-AIKJ, G-AKWJ, G-AKXK, G-AMGE, G-ANGB**
Proctor 4:	G-AKYJ, G-ANYC, TF-OSK
Proctor 5:	G-AHGL, G-AHTK, G-AHWO, G-AHWT (wings only), G-AKYB (wings only), G-ANAT
Provost:	WV605
Scion:	G-AEZF
Sea Prince:	WF119
Tiger Moth:	G-ANCX, G-ANDE, G-ANEW (in pieces), G-ANRA, G-ANRU, G-ANRY, G-ANSG, G-ANYN, G-AOBO, G-AODT, D-EMAX (ex-G-ANJF)
Widgeon (Grumman):	F-BGTD
W/S S.51 Dragonfly:	G-AJOV***

* G-AMYW was fitted with geophysical research equipment, including booms extending rearwards from the tail unit.
** G-ANGB was inscribed with the Olympic Games insignia and was due to fly to Australia. More of the background to the proposed flight is told in the book *"Tails of the Fifties."*
*** G-AJOV was used by the *"Evening News"* and carried a large board on each side proclaiming this (see *"Tail Ends of the Fifties"*).

APPENDIX 11
AIRCRAFT OVERFLYING WOKING ON FAIRLY TYPICAL DAYS DURING THE MID-FIFTIES

Noted in order of their being seen during the day.

WEDNESDAY 11TH AUGUST 1954
C-47:	14838
Valiant 2:	WJ954
Dakota 3:	G-AGHP
DC-4:	F-BELP
Dove 1:	G-AKSV
Aiglet Tr. J/5F:	G-AMTC
Viscount:	G-AMOJ
Tiger Moth:	G-ALJA
Autocrat J/1:	G-AJDV
Viscount:	G-AMNZ
Bristol 171:	G-AMWH
Hastings:	WD480
Viscount:	F-BGNR
Hawk Tr. 3:	G-ALUX
Heron 1:	G-ANNO
DC-4:	F-BELF
C-47A:	EI-ACH
Moth Minor:	G-AFOZ
Taylorcraft Plus D:	G-AIXB
DC-4:	F-BELN
Bristol 170 Mk.21:	G-AGVC
Viking 1:	G-AHOW
Autocrat J/1:	G-AHCK
Tiger Moth:	G-ANDG

Also seen but unidentified:
DC-3 of Air Service Training
Oxford
Prentice
Meteor
S.51 of Royal Navy

FRIDAY 29TH APRIL 1955
Harvard:	KF729
Dakota 3:	G-AGJZ
C-47:	ZU-6
Canberra:	WD935
Vampire FB.5:	WA121
Proctor 1:	G-AHVA
Anson 11:	PH788
Dart-Dakota:	G-AMDB
DC-6:	LV-ADS
Autocrat J/1:	G-AGXH
DC-4:	EC-ACF
Argonaut:	G-ALHJ
Viking 1:	G-AMNK
Argonaut:	G-ALHD
Bristol 170 Mk. 32:	G-AMWD

Tiger Moth:	G-ANDF
Viscount:	G-AMOO
Ashton:	WB494
Dragon Rapide:	G-AJHP
Autocrat J/1:	G-AIGU
Viscount:	G-ANRR
Dragon Rapide:	G-AGDM
Bonanza:	G-AOAM
Devon:	VP975

Also seen but unidentified:
Catalina
Thunderjet
Meteor NF.14

WEDNESDAY 4TH APRIL 1956

Consul:	G-AIKT
Dove 1:	G-AKSV
Devon:	VP957
Constellation:	ZS-DBT
Convair-Liner:	HB-IRP
Ambassador:	G-ALZR
Dakota 3:	G-ALXM
Tiger Moth:	G-ANPB
Viscount 708:	F-BGNN
Hornet Moth:	G-AHBL
Valiant:	WZ382
Anson 19:	TX226
Auster 5:	G-ANRP
Constellation:	G-ALAN
Proctor 1:	G-AHVA
Tiger Moth:	G-ANDV
Valiant:	WZ390
Valiant:	WP210
Constellation:	G-ANVD
Victor:	WB775

WEDNESDAY 21ST AUGUST 1957

Dove 1:	G-AKSV
Scimitar:	WT333
C-119 Packet:	IK461
DC-3:	HB-IRL
Chipmunk:	G-AORL
Viscount 700:	G-AMAV
Lincoln:	SX944
Convair-Liner:	HB-IMG
Superconstellation:	VT-DIM
Tiger Moth:	G-AIJA
DC-6B:	N6532C
Viscount:	PH-VIC
Tiger Moth:	G-AODU
Dragon Rapide:	G-AHED
DC-6:	N5027K
Dragon Rapide:	G-AJHP
Anson 21:	VS562
Anson 21:	VV907

Stratocruiser:	G-ALSD
Constellation:	G-ANVB
Stratocruiser:	G-ANTY
Alpine:	G-APAA
Dakota 3:	G-AGIU
Dakota 3:	G-AGZC
Tiger Moth:	G-AOAC
Convair-Liner:	HB-IMP
DC-6B:	HB-IBI
Prince:	G-AMLZ
Proctor 3:	G-AHFK
Tiger Moth:	G-AHRM

WEDNESDAY 2ND APRIL 1958

Viscount:	VT-DIZ (low runs)
Dragon Rapide:	G-AHJA
Dragon Rapide:	G-AJSL
Alpha J/1N:	G-AJIS
Chipmunk:	WZ875
Viscount:	EP-AHA
Heron 2:	G-AOGW
Gemini 1A:	G-AJWF
Britannia:	G-APLL
Dove 1:	G-ANVC
Hawk Tr. 3:	G-AKKR
Sea Balliol:	WL734
Vulcan:	XA890
Alpha J/1N:	G-AGTP
Viscount:	G-AOYV
Dragon Rapide:	G-AHKB
Auster 3:	G-AHLK
Constellation:	PH-LDG
Dove 2B:	G-AMDD
Scimitar:	WW134

Also seen but unidentified:
Beverley x 3
Meteor
Anson x 2
Packet
Noratlas
Globemaster

APPENDIX 12
AIRCRAFT AT THE WOBURN RALLY, MAY 2ND 1959

Aeronca 100:	G-AEVS
Apache:	G-APCL
Argus:	G-AJPI
Autocrat J/1:	G-AGVG, G-AGXB, G-AGYD, G-AGYP, G-AHAM, G-AHHM, G-AHHP, G-AIRB, G-AIZU, G-AJAE
Alpha J/1N:	G-AGXH (overflight), G-AHCN, G-AHHU, G-AIGM, G-AJEB, G-AOXR
Arrow J/2:	G-AJAM
Auster J/4:	G-AIJK, G-APJM
Aiglet Tr. J/5F:	G-AMTA, G-AMTB
Aiglet Tr. J/5L:	G-AOFS
Alpine J/5R:	G-AOGV, G-APCX
Auster 5:	G-ANIE, G-APAH, G-APJX
Auster 5D:	G-AGLK
Belfair:	G-AOXO, G-APIE
Chipmunk:	G-AOPZ, G-AOTM, G-AOZV
Cub Coupé:	G-AFSZ
Dragon Rapide:	G-AGJG, G-AHGD (damaged when landing), G-AHJS, G-AHKB, G-AHKV
GAL.42 Cygnet:	G-AFVR
Gemini 1A:	G-AJZS, G-AKDD, G-AKEM, G-AKER, G-AKGD, G-AKHK, G-ALUG
Gemini 3C:	G-ALZG
Gemini 7:	G-AKHZ
Hawk Tr. 3:	G-AFBS
Hornet Moth:	G-ADKK, G-ADNB, G-ADND, G-ADOT, G-ADSK, G-AEET, G-AHBL, G-AMZO
Jackaroo:	G-ANZT, G-AOIR, G-APAJ, G-APAO
Leopard Moth:	G-AIYS
Linnet:	G-APNS
Messenger 2A:	G-AGPX, G-AHZT, G-AIEK, G-AJDM, G-AKIR, G-AKKO
Monarch:	G-AFJU
Motor Tutor:	G-AKJD
Nipper:	OO-NIF
Prentice:	G-AONB
Proctor 1:	G-AIED, G-AIHG
Proctor 2:	G-AIEH
Proctor 5:	G-AIET
Prospector:	XM397 (overflight)
Pup:	N5180
Swallow 2:	G-AEMW
Swift:	G-AHWH
Taylorcraft Plus D:	G-AFWO, G-AFZI, G-AHCG
Tiger Moth:	G-AHVU, G-AHXN, G-ALWW, G-ANEH, G-ANIY, G-ANOD, G-ANOH, G-ANRF, G-ANUE, G-APKE, G-APRA
Tipsy Tr.:	G-AFRV
Turbulent:	G-AJCP, G-APBZ, G-APIZ, G-APKZ
Turbi:	G-AOTK
Vega Gull:	G-AHET

APPENDIX 13
AIRCRAFT AT THE GOODWOOD MOTOR RACING MEETING, APRIL 18TH 1960

Aero 45:	G-APRR
Apache:	G-APFV
Autocrat J/1:	G-AGVL, G-AHHS, G-AIBX, G-AJIH, G-AJIT, G-AJRC
Alpha J/1N:	G-AGTP, G-AGXH, G-AHSO, G-AIGT, G-AIGU, G-AIJI, G-AJIW
Aiglet Tr. J/5F:	G-AMTB, G-AMTD, G-AMTR
Autocar J/5P:	G-AOHZ, G-APKI
Auster D.4:	G-25-8
Auster 4:	G-ANHU
Auster 5:	G-AKXP, G-ANHU, G-APBW, G-APJX
Auster 5D:	G-ANHW, G-AOUL
Bonanza:	EI-ALL
Caribbean:	G-APXS
Cessna 150:	G-APXY
Cessna 172:	G-APSZ
Cessna 175:	G-APYA, G-APYM
Cessna 210:	N7307E
Cessna 310:	G-APUF
Chipmunk:	G-AORK, G-AORL, G-AOSN, G-AOSO, G-AOTM, G-APOE, G-APOY, G-APSC
Comanche:	G-APZG
Commander:	N2718A
Cub Coupé:	G-AFSZ
Dove 2:	G-AKJG
Dove 6:	G-ANGU
Dragon Rapide:	G-AJSL, G-AKNN, G-AKNY
Gemini 1A:	G-AJKS, G-AJZS, G-AKEL, G-AKHB, G-AKHP
Gemini 3A:	G-AKHC, G-ALMU
Hawk Tr. 3:	G-AFBS, G-ALUX
Hornet Moth:	G-ADKL, G-AMZO
Hurricane:	PZ865 (G-AMAU) (display)
Jackaroo:	G-AOEX
Jodel D.117:	G-APOZ
Leopard Moth:	G-ACMN, G-AIYS
Linnet:	G-APNS
Messenger 2A:	G-AGPX, G-AJDF, G-AJDM, G-AKKC
Messenger 4A:	G-AKZX, G-ALAP
Meta Sokol:	G-APVU
Monarch:	G-AFJU
Piaggio P.166:	G-APSJ
Prentice:	G-APIY
Proctor 1:	G-AHNA, G-AHVA
Proctor 3:	G-ALES
Proctor 4:	G-AOBI
Proctor 5:	G-AHGL, G-AIAF
Prospector:	G-AOZO
Spitfire:	AB910 (display)
Super Cub:	G-APZJ
Swallow 2:	G-AFCL, G-AFHS

Taylorcraft Plus D:	G-AHSD
Tiger Moth:	G-AHIZ, G-ALND, G-AMHF, G-ANSR, G-ANUD, G-AOEI, G-AOEL, G-AOGS, G-AOZH, G-APJL
Tripacer:	G-APVA, G-APXM, G-APYI, G-APYW, D-EHAS, EI-AKY
Turbulent:	G-AJCP, G-APYZ
Vega Gull:	G-AEYC

APPENDIX 14
TIGER CLUB AIRCRAFT SEEN AT FAIR OAKS DURING 1957

All silver overall with coloured registration, fin and cowling.

G-ACDC	Tiger Moth	silver wings & red fuselage (the exception)	
G-ANEB	Tiger Moth	silver & cream	
G-ANHI	Tiger Moth	silver & eau de nil	No. 28
G-ANKH	Tiger Moth	silver & red	
G-ANKY	Tiger Moth	silver & blue	
G-ANLB	Tiger Moth	silver & black	
G-ANSH	Tiger Moth	silver & green	No. 24
G-ANZY	Tiger Moth		
G-ANZZ	Tiger Moth	silver & blue	No. 22
G-AOAA	Tiger Moth	silver & blue/red	No. 23
G-AOAB	Tiger Moth	silver & green	No. 27
G-AOAD	Tiger Moth	silver & orange stripes	No. 26
G-AODR	Tiger Moth	silver & blue	No. 25
G-AOXS	Tiger Moth	silver & green	
G-AORY	Tiger Moth	silver & orange	
G-AOZB	Tiger Moth		
G-AOZC	Tiger Moth		
G-APAY	Tiger Moth	silver & turquoise	
G-APCC	Tiger Moth	silver & green	

APPENDIX 15
AIRCRAFT PARTICIPATING IN THE FIRST TIGER CLUB AIRSHOW AT FAIR OAKS, 19TH JULY 1958

G-ACDC	Tiger Moth
G-ADNB	Hornet Moth
G-AEBJ	Blackburn B-2
G-AEWV	Aeronca 100
G-AHHU	Autocrat
G-AKJD	Motor Tutor
G-ANFI	Tiger Moth
G-ANHI	Tiger Moth
G-ANSH	Tiger Moth
G-ANZZ	Tiger Moth
G-AOAA	Tiger Moth
G-AODR	Tiger Moth
G-AOEX	Tiger Moth
G-AOIR	Tiger Moth
G-AOXS	Tiger Moth
G-APAI	Tiger Moth
G-APDZ	Tiger Moth
G-APBZ	Turbulent
G-APIZ	Turbulent
G-APKZ	Turbulent
AB910	Spitfire (displayed but did not land)
VF544	Auster AOP.6

APPENDIX 16
AIRCRAFT FLOWN IN BY AUTHOR BETWEEN 1950 AND 1965

NF854	Dominie	Lee-on-Solent	summer 1950
G-AHSO	Autocrat	Fair Oaks	18/08/52
G-AHSO	Autocrat	Fair Oaks	11/12/52
MH117	Anson 1	Ford	13/06/53
PH606	Anson 11	Shoreham	17/07/53
WK556	Chipmunk	Cranwell	27/07/53
WK567	Chipmunk	Cranwell	28/07/53
PH528	Anson 11	Shoreham	02/07/54
G-ANAL	W/S S.51	Croydon	18/07/54
G-ALUX	Hawk Tr. 3	Fair Oaks	27/12/54
G-AOAM	Bonanza	Fair Oaks	31/07/55
G-AKUW	Super Ace	Fair Oaks-White Waltham-Fair Oaks	18/09/55
G-AELO	Hornet Moth	Croydon-Shoreham-Fair Oaks	20/09/55
G-AHSO	Autocrat	Fair Oaks	30/10/55
WZ796	Grasshopper	Lancing	18/11/55
G-ANUD	Tiger Moth	Fair Oaks	15/04/56
G-AOAC	Tiger Moth	Fair Oaks	01/06/57
G-ANUD	Tiger Moth	Fair Oaks-Shoreham-Fair Oaks	24/07/57
G-AIGU	Autocrat	Fair Oaks	17/09/57
G-AIGU	Autocrat	Fair Oaks	19/09/57
G-AJOA	Tiger Moth	Fair Oaks	23/02/58
G-AIGU	Alpha	Fair Oaks	10/05/58
G-AIGU	Alpha	Fair Oaks	01/06/58
G-AOCR	Auster 5D	Fair Oaks	17/06/58
G-AJDV	Alpha	Fair Oaks	20/06/58
G-AJDV	Alpha	Fair Oaks	05/08/58
G-AHLJ	Taylorcraft Plus D	Fair Oaks	06/08/58
G-AIVO	Viking 1B	Blackbushe-Brussels-Blackbushe	23/09/58
G-APHU	Auster 5	Fair Oaks	30/03/59
G-AJDV	Alpha	Fair Oaks	03/08/59
G-AJDV	Alpha	Fair Oaks	28/08/59
G-AODS	Tiger Moth	Fair Oaks	20/09/59
G-AHLJ	Taylorcraft Plus D	Fair Oaks	29/09/59
G-AJDV	Alpha	Fair Oaks	16/04/60
G-APXS	Caribbean	Shoreham	21/05/60
G-APBE	Auster 5	Biggin Hill	26/12/60
G-APXO	Caribbean	Fair Oaks	18/03/61
G-AORL	Chipmunk	Fair Oaks	27/04/61
G-APXO	Caribbean	Fair Oaks	07/05/61
G-AGXT	Alpha	Elstree	18/06/61
G-AJDV	Alpha	Fair Oaks	09/07/61
G-AMAD	Ambassador	Heathrow-Woolsington	08/08/61
G-AGVF	Alpha	Plymouth	24/08/61
G-APXO	Caribbean	Fair Oaks-Shoreham-Fair Oaks	28/10/61
G-AROD	Cessna 175	Fair Oaks-Redhill-Fair Oaks	24/03/62
G-AOAC	Tiger Moth	Fair Oaks	29/04/62
G-APKL	Alpha	Blackbushe-Eastleigh-Blackbushe	29/07/62
G-ANHR	Auster 5	Shoreham	19/08/62
G-ARKM	Colt	Fair Oaks-Blackbushe-Fair Oaks	14/04/63
G-ADDI	Dragon	Rochester	07/09/63
G-AGVF	Alpha	Plymouth	24/09/63

G-AROW	Mousquetaire	Fair Oaks	12/10/63
G-APCY	Alpha	Blackbushe	10/11/63
G-ASFW	Linnet	Blackbushe	29/12/63
G-ASFW	Linnet	Blackbushe	26/01/64
G-ASFW	Linnet	Blackbushe	02/02/64
G-ASFW	Linnet	Blackbushe	09/02/94
G-AJYB	Alpha	Compton Abbas	25/05/64
G-ASCZ	Emeraude	Blackbushe	17/06/64
G-ASFW	Linnet	Blackbushe	25/07/64
G-AOHF	Autocar	Blackbushe	05/09/64
G-AJEH	Alpha	Compton Abbas	28/03/65
G-ASNL	Sikorsky S.61N	Penzance-St. Mary's	30/03/65
G-ASNL	Sikorsky S.61N	St. Mary's-Penzance	01/04/65
G-ALYD	Auster 5	Blackbushe	01/05/65
G-ASUZ	Heron 2D	Gatwick-Swansea-Gatwick	02/09/65

INDEX (Main Text Only)

A
A30	95, 97
A35	95, 97, 102
A40 Devon	94
A40 Farina	91, 97
A40 Somerset	94
ACTIVE, ARROW	84
Admiralty	14
Adur, River	44
AERONCA 100	87
"Aeroplane, The"	50, 81
AEROVAN	41, 50, 59, 65, 83, 96
AIGLET TRAINER	60, 85
Air Experience Flight	54, 60
Air Ministry	19
Air Service Training	53
Air Traffic Control	44, 59, 82
Air-Britain	10, 42
Airspeed	49
Airways Aero Associations	52, 60
Aldgate	71
Allen-Mills AM-10	81
ALPHA	83, 85
Alpine Ices	51
ALPINE	85
Alston, John	67
Alton	97
Amos, Peter	48
Anderson Shelter	14
Andover	94-6
Anglia, Ford	98
Ansell, Philip	48, 59
ANSON	32, 45, 49, 54, 60, 61, 64, 80
APACHE	103
Arctic Circle	84
ARGONAUT	80
ARGUS, FAIRCHILD	86
ARIES	61
Armstrong, Louis	9
Army	19, 45, 60
Army Air Corps	58
Arnold, Doug	82
ARROW, SPARTAN	45, 64
Arthur, WingCo	83-5
Astaire, Fred	25
Aston Down	61
Atherton, Mr	61
Atomium	95
ATTACKER	53
AUSTER	21, 45, 48, 52, 53, 61, 62, 65, 69, 73, 83, 85, 89, 102, 103
Austin Eight	11, 90
Austin Seven	11, 94-8
Austin Six	94
AUTOCRAT	47, 48, 59, 61
Automobile Association	85
AVENGER	53

B
B-29	15
Bader, Douglas	61
Baggy Point	71
Baginton (Coventry)	49, 94
BALLIOL	48
Bancroft, Dennis	51
Bank Station	71
Banner-Towing	53, 65
Barber, Ambrose	82
Barber, Mr	61
Barmouth	18
Barney, Mick	89
Barwell, David	55
Bath	14
BEA	50, 98, 101
Beagle Aircraft	45
BEAVER	65
Beeching, Dr	34
Bees Flight	48
Bell, Eric	65
Bells of Surbiton	90
Bembridge	48
Benjamin, Lewis	84
Bertram Mills Circus	31
Betjeman, John	55
Beverley Sisters	28
BEVERLEY	49
Bicycle	34, 42, 48, 50, 87
Blackbushe	10, 64, 94, 95
Black Gang	30
Bloodnok, Major	54
Bluebottle	54, 71
Board of Trade	95
Bognor Regis	53
Boiler Hill	40, 41
BONANZA	82
Boscombe Down	94, 95, 98
Boston	47
'Bradshaw'	84
Brand, Mr	36
Brighton Racecourse	53
Brighton	19, 34, 53
"British Civil Aviation News"	88
British Precision Flying Team	85
British Rail	72
Brooklands	80
Brown, Don	50, 60

Browning, Neville	87	Copping, Brian	90
Bruin, Mrs	33	Coronation Fly-Past	46
Brunicardi, Mr	64	Cors-y-Gedol	18, 25, 30
Brussels Exhibition	95	Cottesmore School	17, 25, 28, 30,
Buchan Hill	19-21, 25, 28, 30		31, 33, 42, 100
Buckberry, Jean	47	*"Cottesmorian, The"*	20
Buckingham, Jim	49	**Courtley, Bert**	92
Bunsen Burner	36	*Coventry (Baginton)*	49, 94
Butlins, Filey	68	**Coward, Nöel**	25
		Cox, Ben	50
C		*Cranfield*	103
Cadets	41, 45, 56, 68, 69	Cranwell Passing Out Parade	46
Callingham, Lance	27	*Cranwell*	46, 47, 99
Campbell, Bessie	15	**Crawford, Peter**	25
Campbell, Harold Gordon	13	Crawley New Town	29
Campbell, Honor	86, 102	**Creevy, Mike**	89
Campbell, James	103	"Critical Mass"	74-5
Campbell, Violet	13	**Cromwell, Oliver**	18
CANBERRA	73, 80	Cross Country Running	25, 35, 42
Cane, The	8, 24, 35	**Crown Prince of Iraq**	80
Carlyle, Mr T.	59	Crown, The (Chertsey)	91
Cass, Sir John (College)	70, 71	Croyde Bay	72
"Cassowary"	73, 75	Croydon Flying Club	52
CESSNA	103	*Croydon*	48, 52, 54, 60, 61,
Challis, Mr	65		65-67, 69, 82, 90
CHAMPION, AERONCA	45	"Crundon University"	75
Channel Islands	101	CUB COUPÉ	61
Chapel	20, 34, 37, 39, 44, 51, 68	CUB, PIPER	45
Chemistry	35, 57, 66, 70, 72, 73, 75-7, 96	Cuba Missile Crisis	104
"Chemistry and the Aeroplane"	66	*Culdrose*	96
CHEROKEE ARROW	45	CYGNET, HAWKER	80
Chertsey	86, 91		
Chilbolton	95	**D**	
CHILTON	45, 87	*"Daily Mirror"*	102
CHIPMUNK	32, 47, 48, 53,	Dance, School	38
	60, 64, 82, 86	Dancing Classes	38
Chivenor	68, 72, 95, 96	**Dancy, John**	58
"Chobham Chaser"	87	**Davison-Brown, Col.**	17
Chobham Clumps & Common	82	**Dawson, Les**	73
Christchurch	52, 95, 96	DC-3	22, 48, 53, 80, 98, 101
Christchurch Aero Club	52	DC-4	80
Circle Line	72	DC-6	80
"Civil Aircraft Markings"	11	de Havilland	45, 59, 65, 103
(Ian Allan)		*Denham*	52, 61, 64, 95
Clark, Mr	65	**Dennison, Mr**	64
Clarke, Roger	99	*Derby*	64
Cobbett, Bill	87	**Derry, Wilf**	37
Cobbett, Ted	83	Devonair	96
Cogan, Alma	67	Diamond	21
Colerne	96	'Diamond Lil'	83
COMANCHE	103	Dinky Toys	15
COMET, DH.88	32	*Dishforth*	61
Conry, Mike	65	**Docker, Sir Bernard & Lady**	29
CONSTELLATION	80	DOMINIE	32, 64
Cooper, Mr	61	Don Everall Aviation	53

Donald, Keith	48	FIREFLY	48, 53
DOODLEBUG	14, 15	**Fitzgerald, Ella**	90
Donaldson, Gp. Capt.	31	"Five Got Rhythm"	68
Dorset Foods	103	*"Flight"*	70, 85, 87
DOVE	48, 52, 59-61, 64, 81	Flight Sergeant	45, 69
Dovell, Bill	45, 55, 56, 69	Flightways	53
DRAGON RAPIDE	22, 32, 48, 52, 53, 59, 61, 67, 80, 81, 85	*"Flyer"*	45
		Flying Saucer Day	88
DRAGONFLY (DH)	86	Flying Scholarship	83, 99
DRAGONFLY (S.51)	46, 53	Food	14, 20, 24, 35, 46, 75, 91, 102, 103
"Drain, The"	71	**Forbes, Ian**	61, 65
Drake, Chris	95	Ford RNVR Flying Group	52
"Duck Pond"	23	*Ford, RNAS*	45, 52, 53, 56
Dunkerley, Fred	49	**Foster, Tim**	9, 42, 51, 82, 102
Dunkerley, Kathleen	50	"Four Friends, The"	89
Dunsfold	34, 80	**Fox, Colonel**	82
Dyffryn	18	Fox's Glacier Mints	65
Dykes	35, 42	FREIGHTER, BRISTOL	48

E

G

Earls Court	31	Gala Cosmetics	102
East Anglian Flying Services	52, 59-61	GANNET	53
Eastleigh	52, 65, 94, 96, 98, 101	**Garland, Judy**	25, 89
Eccles	54, 71	**Garner, Erroll**	90
Eclipse of the Sun	53	*Gatwick*	21, 48, 52, 100
ED "Bee"	81	GCE 'A' Level Exams	57-9, 66, 70
ED "Hornet"	81	GEMINI	47, 53, 59, 61, 64, 85, 103
Edinburgh	13	**George VI, King**	19
Edinburgh, Duke of	46, 64	Gipsy Major	52
Elmdon	57, 65	Glandular Fever	57, 66
Eltham	48	Godalming	94
Emery, Dick	86	*Goodwood Circuit*	100
Emney, Fred	49	Goodyear Trophy Air Race	49, 54
"Enola Gay"	15	"Goon Show, The"	54, 71
Evacuee	14, 48	Gosport Tube	83
"Evening Standard"	53, 54, 68, 72	**Granz, Norman**	90
Exeter	95-7	GRASSHOPPER, SLINGSBY	69
Experimental Flying Group	52, 82, 85	Great Vintage Flying Weekend	96
EXPRESS (DH.86)	22	**Grece, Wing Commander**	47
		Green, John	17, 31

F

		Gritpype-Thynne	54
"Facing the Paint"	24-5	**Grummett, David**	70
Fairoaks vs. Fair Oaks	14, 82, 84	*Guernsey*	59, 60
Fair Oaks	32, 42, 52, 56, 61, 67, 80-88, 103	GUGNUNC, HANDLEY PAGE	87
		Guildford Technical College	70, 86, 94
FAIREY	60	Guildford	33, 83, 86, 92, 97
Fairfield Halls	90		
Fairthorpe Electron Minor	95	**H**	
FALCON SIX	49	**Habgood, Tony**	56
Farmer, Dudley	19, 20	**Hailey, Bill**	72
Farnborough	51, 53, 56, 59, 94, 95	*Hamble*	95
Festival of Britain	8, 32	Hampshire Aeroplane Club	52, 98, 101
Fieldwick, Bernie	61	Hampton Court	91
"Fifties Revisited, The"	104	**Harness, Charlie**	73
Filton	95	HARRIER	64

HARVARD	60		
Haselmere	84	**K**	
Hatfield	65, 95	**Keeling, Peter**	50, 54, 55, 99
HAWK TRAINER	49, 52, 56, 59-61, 73, 82, 84, 86	*Keevil*	96
		Kendall, Hugh	50
Hawker Aircraft	34, 80	*Kenley*	54
Hawthorne, Mike	86	**Kennedy, Hugh**	53
Hayes, Tubby	91	**Kenton, Stan**	90
Hayhow, Tom	85	*Kidlington*	103
Heath, Ted	89	**Kilshaw, Cindy**	89
Heathrow	50, 67, 80, 95, 102, 103	King's College, London	13
Hendon	21, 65	King's Cup Air Race	49, 85, 94
Henstridge	94	KITTEN, DART	45
HERALD	49	'Klondyke Kate'	83
HERON	81, 98	**Kunz, Charlie**	89
Hibberson, Mr	66		
Hilder, Alan	25	**L**	
Hill, John	51	Lambert, Mark	87
Hiroshima	15	Lamtex Rugs	53
Höhner Electric Piano	91	Lancing College	7, 9, 31, 33-35, 39, 40, 44, 46, 68, 70, 83, 90
Honner, Joyce	14, 31, 48		
Hookwood Flying Group	52	Langley	80
Hornby-Dublo	17, 39	Leadenhall Street	71
HORNET MOTH	52, 61, 65, 67	**Lecomber, Brian**	87
Horsell Common	14	*Lee-on-Solent*	31, 64
Horsham	33	**Lehrer, Tom**	89
Hove Grammar School	98	*Leicester*	64
Hove	17, 19, 20, 25, 30, 42, 98, 99	**Leigh, Vivien**	27
Hucknall	64	LINCOLN	46, 53
HUNTER	73	LINNET	10
HUREL DUBOIS HD.31	48, 50	"Lion Works, The"	92
Hurn	95, 96	*Llanbedr*	18
HURRICANE	80	London Aero Club	52
		London Transport Flying Club	85
I		London University Fashion Show	73
Iceland	69	London	13, 14, 19, 31, 46, 48, 49, 52, 55, 67, 68, 70, 71, 73, 85, 90, 91, 95, 102
"In and out of School"	18		
Ipplepen	97		
Ipswich	59, 61	**Lotis, Dennis**	67
Island Airways	67	**Lucas, Mr**	65
Isle of Wight	48	**Lynn, Fred**	48
J		**M**	
Jagger, Sam	35, 42, 58	M.52	50
Jazz Ball	92	**Mair, Alex**	87
Jazz	89-92	**Mallinson, Peter**	70
Jersey Airlines	98	*Manston*	64
Jersey	59,61	**Manuel, Mr L.W.**	88
Jetex	81	Maps	40-2
Johnson, Colin	33	MARATHON	53
Johnston, Mr J.R.	61, 84	**Marks, Peter**	90, 93
Jones, "Mike"	70, 82, 94, 95	**Marshall, "Tiny"**	60
Jones, Michael	103	Marshall's Flying Services	53
Jones, Norman	86	**Martin, Bernard**	88
Jungle Patrol	30	**Martin, David**	50

Martin, Dean	68	Newlands Corner Hotel	92
Martin, Howard	55	Newlands Primary School	98
Martin, Mr	65	NIGHTHAWK	47
Masefield, Peter	86	Nightscale Flying Services	52
Maskelyne & Devant	31	"No Highway"	40
Matthews, Tom	90	North Devon	72, 73
McDonald, Mr	65	North Downs	72
McDonnell, Capt.	61		
McKay, Alistair	89	**O**	
Meldon	72	**Oakden, "Nurse"**	26
Memory Training	78	Oakeley Arms Hotel	18
Mercedes	101	*Old Sarum*	94
Meridian Airmaps	41, 59	**Olivier, Laurence**	27
Merrow	85	**Olivier, Tarquin**	27
Merryfield	96	Olympic Games, 1948	31
MESSENGER	52, 56, 59, 64, 69	"One Hundred Years of Cottesmore"	25, 30
METEOR	16, 53, 64, 73		
Methylated Spirits	35	**Ord-Hume, Arthur**	88
MEW GULL	49	Orkney Islands	13
Midas Club	91		
Middle Wallop	52, 60, 94-6	**P**	
Midland Flying Club	59	Paddington	18, 51
"Miles Aircraft since 1925"	51, 66	**Paine, "Buster"**	64
Miles Biro Pen	26	**Paine, Ron**	61
Miles, F.G. Ltd	50, 56, 58, 59, 61, 66, 103	Panshanger	52, 95
		Paris (Le Bourget)	59, 61
Miles, George	38, 49, 58, 64, 65	**Pashley, Cecil**	60, 66
Milk Marketing Board	91, 98, 102	**Pashley, Vera**	66
Miller, Mark	67	"Passport to Freedom"	27
Milligan, Spike	9, 104	Pearl Assurance Company	21
Minic Toys	15	**Pearse-Smith, Mr**	65
Mitchell, Yvonne	60	Pease Pottage	19
Model Aeroplanes	17, 22, 39, 49, 70, 81, 82	**Pelham, Henry**	87
		Penguin Flying Club	52
Model Railways	17, 22, 39	**Penrose, Harald**	87
Moelfre	18, 19	PERCIVAL	45, 49, 103
Moll, Gerry	20, 22, 25	**Peters, John**	22, 31
MONARCH	49	**Peterson, Oscar**	89, 90
Morecambe & Wise	73	PIPER	45, 103
"More Tails of the Fifties"	88	"Piperama"	103
Moriarty	54	'Pleasure'	36
Morris 1000	86, 94	*Plymouth*	95, 96
Morris Eight	25	Pooh Bear	73
MOTH, DH	65	Porlock Hill	96
Murray, Ruby	68	**Porteous, Ranald**	88
Museum of Berkshire Aviation	39, 49	*Portland*	96
Music	38, 67, 68, 73, 86, 89-93, 97	Portsmouth	52, 59, 61, 71, 82, 84, 95
Musselburgh	13	Potato Saga	28-9
		Powell, Bob	97
N		Powerjets	51
Nash Aero Collection	50	PRENTICE	53, 95, 102
NAVION	69	**Previn, André**	73
"Nelson"	71	PRINCE	48, 65
Newark Air Museum	64	**Princess Elizabeth**	29
Newbury	11	PRINCESS, SAUNDERS ROE	48

"Private Eye"	73
PROCTOR	44, 61, 64, 65, 69, 103
PROVOST	48
Pursey, Mr H.B.	59

Q
Queen Elizabeth College	73

R
Radio Luxembourg	67
Radlett	95
Ranmore Common	61
RB.108	64
Read, Al	53
Red Arrows	70, 87
Redhill	52
Reid, John	65
Renshaw, John	90
Rhoose	65
Riddle, Nelson	89
"Right Monkey"	53
"Riverside Quartet, The"	90
Rochester	52, 59
Rogers, Elaine	94
Rogerson, Marion	20
Rogerson, Mark	20, 25
Rogerson, Michael	18, 19, 20
Rockets	76, 81
Rolls Royce	64, 84
Rose, Nick	51, 55
ROTOCYCLE, HILLER	98
RAeS Garden Party	86
Royal Artillery Aero Club	52
Royal Naval Flying Club	52
Ryde	48

S
Saillard, Mr	21
Saints' Days	40, 48
"Salad Days"	72
Sandown	48
Saunders Roe	46, 48, 98, 101
Schöenberg	73
Science Museum	87
SCIMITAR	80
SEA BALLIOL	53
SEA FURY	53
SEA HAWK	53
SEA HORNET	48
SEA PRINCE	53
SEAFIRE	48
Seagoon, Neddie	54, 71
Sellotape	26-7
Shackleton (W.S.) Weekend	10, 96
Shaftesbury	102

Shapinsay	13
Shipp, Bert	90
Shoreham	33, 34, 40-42, 44
Shoreham Airport	7, 9, 41-46, 48-50, 52-57, 59-61, 66-68, 70, 82-84, 98
Short Bros & Harland Flying Club	52
SHORT SC.1	64
Sidcot Suit	60
SIKORSKY S.51	54
Silvester, Victor	38
Simmons, Jean	54
Sinatra, Frank	56, 89
SKEETER	69, 98, 101
Skegness	47
'SKYBIKE'	88
Slade, Julian	72
Slinfold	11
Smith, Alan	90
Smoke Mixture	77
Snook, Len	82
Sociability Index	100
"Social Development of Adolescents"	99
"Sound Barrier, The"	40, 85
"Soup, Seven and Six"	36
Southampton Hall of Aviation	81
South Downs	34
Southend	52, 59-61, 102
Southern Aero Club	52, 59, 60, 66
Southern Flying Schools	52
South Marston	80
South Shields	15
SPARROWHAWK	49, 50
SPARROWJET	49, 67
Speechly, Mr	65
SPITFIRE	14, 15
Sponphony	92
Sproule, Lt. Cdr.	46
SPUTNIK	104
St. Benet's	13
St. Eval	96
St. Just	96
St. Mawgan	96
Steele, Mike	55
Steyning	44, 83
"Steyning Flier"	33
STRATOCRUISER	80
Strawberries and Cream	36
STUDENT	83
Students' Union	73
Studio 51	53
Summer Camps	46, 48, 60
"Suntan with Nylon"	53
SUPER ACE	82
SUPER CUB	103

SUPERFREIGHTER	98, 101	**W**	
Surrey Aviation	52, 60, 66	Walker, James & Sons	92
Sussex Pad Hotel	51	**Wallace, Ian**	55
SWALLOW, BA	45	**Wallis, Barnes**	66
Sweden	69	**Walton, Dave**	76
Sywell	10	**Warburton, Major**	60
		"War of the Worlds"	14
T		WASHINGTON (B-50)	80
"Tail Ends of the Fifties"	47	WASP	101
"Tails of the Fifties"	61, 65, 86, 87	Waterloo	71, 72, 84
Tangmere	53	WELLINGTON	80
Tan-y-Bwlch	18	**Wells, H.G.**	14
Tarrant Rushton	65, 95	Wembley	31
TAYLORCRAFT PLUS D	10	West Byfleet	87, 102
Thorney Island	53	**Westbrook, Mr E.W.**	59
Thorold, Henry	36	*Weston Zoyland*	95
Three Counties Flying Club	10	*Weston-super-Mare*	95, 96
Thruxton	52, 94-6	Westward Ho!	72
Tiger Club, The	84, 86, 103	Weybridge	66, 81
TIGER MOTH	9, 52, 59, 62, 82-85, 87	**Whellem, Capt.**	60
Tilbury, Ann	70, 72, 87	*White Waltham*	52, 60, 64, 82
Timmis, Alexander	83	**White, "Chalky"**	93
Timmis, David	17, 32, 51, 68, 83, 86, 102	**White, Jean**	93
		White, Richard	89
Tin Pan Alley	68	WHITNEY STRAIGHT	56, 80
Tinsley Green	100	Williams of Hounslow	102
TOMTIT	80	**Williams, Alun**	27
Totnes	96	**Williams, Brook**	27, 100
Trafalgar Square	77	**Wilson, Mike**	70
Trefgarne, Lord	86	Wiltshire School of Flying	52
TRIPACER	103	Winchester College	33
Twickenham	31	Windsor Castle	82
TWIN PIONEER	69	Windsor Park School	13
"Two Grades of Pete"	92	**Wings, Ramon H.**	78, 79
		Wisley	80, 81, 85, 86
U		Witley Pantomime Company	93, 97
Universal Flying Services	32, 52, 83	Wittering	31
Upavon	50, 95, 96	Woburn Rally	96
Usworth	61	Woking	13, 14, 25, 33, 71, 80, 87, 89-92, 95, 97, 98, 102
V		*Woodley*	91, 103
Valentine, Dickie	67	**Woods, Flt. Lt.**	60, 64
VALIANT	80	Woolacombe	72
VAMPIRE TRAINER	53, 56, 99	World Marbles Championship	100
VANGUARD	80	Worthing	33, 40, 42, 44, 54-56, 99
Varcoe, Vivien	64	WOT, CURRIE	98, 101
VARSITY	48, 53, 68	**Wright Brothers**	69
VC.10	80	**Wynn, Humphrey**	87
VEGA GULL	45, 86	WYVERN	53
VICKERS ARMSTRONG	66, 80		
Vigors Aviation	103	**Y**	
VIKING	80, 95	*Yeovil*	94, 96
VISCOUNT	80, 81	*Yeovilton*	94, 96
V-J Day	16	Young Conservatives	86
		Yugoslavia	82, 86

OTHER AVIATION BOOKS WRITTEN OR EDITED BY THIS AUTHOR ARE AVAILABLE DIRECTLY BY MAIL ORDER AS WELL AS THROUGH BOOKSHOPS; THEY INCLUDE THE FOLLOWING:

TAILS OF THE FIFTIES
Compiled and edited by Peter Campbell, published in 1997
(ISBN 0 9515598 3 4)
Price: £11.95 (plus £1.50 p/p if ordered by mail)

MORE TAILS OF THE FIFTIES
Compiled and edited by Peter Campbell, published in 1998
(ISBN 0 9515598 4 2)
Price: £12.95 (plus £1.50 p/p if ordered by mail)

TAIL ENDS OF THE FIFTIES
Compiled and edited by Peter Campbell, published in 1999
(ISBN 0 9515598 9 3)
Price: £12.95 (plus £1.50 p/p if ordered by mail)

SHOREHAM AIRPORT: RECORD OF VISITING AIRCRAFT 1946-1970
By Peter Campbell, first published in 1996, revised in 1998
Price: £5.95 (plus £1.50 p/p if ordered by mail)

FAIR OAKS AERODROME: RECORD OF VISITING AIRCRAFT 1952-1970
By Peter Campbell, first published 1995
Price: £2.00 (plus £0.50 p/p if ordered by mail)

WISLEY AIRFIELD: RECORD OF AIRCRAFT MOVEMENTS 1954-1969
By Peter Campbell, first published 1995
Price: £1.00 (plus £0.50 p/p if ordered by mail)

HAVE YOU WRITTEN A BOOK ABOUT AVIATION THAT YOU WOULD LIKE TO HAVE PUBLISHED? IT IS POSSIBLE THAT WE COULD ARRANGE TO DO THIS FOR YOU AT MINIMAL COST (PRINT RUNS FROM 250 COPIES UPWARDS). IF SO PLEASE CONTACT US.

WHY NOT SEND FOR OUR UNIQUE LIST OF AVIATION BOOKS FROM THE ADDRESS BELOW?

Mail: **Cirrus Associates, Kington Magna, Gillingham, Dorset SP8 5EW**
Telephone/Fax: **01747 838165**
E-Mail: **cirrus@zeugma.force9.co.uk**

Or explore our web site at: **www.zeugma.force9.co.uk/cirrus**